LANDSCAPE
with ROSES

LANDSCAPE
with ROSES

Jeff Cox

Photographs by Jerry Pavia

The Taunton Press

The Taunton Press
Inspiration for hands-on living™

The Taunton Press, Inc., 63 South Main Street, PO Box 5506, Newtown, CT 06470-5506
e-mail: tp@taunton.com

Distributed by Publishers Group West

DESIGNER AND LAYOUT ARTIST: Carol Petro
ILLUSTRATOR: Lainé Roundy
PHOTOGRAPHER: Jerry Pavia

LIBRARY OF CONGRESS CATALOGING-IN-PUBLICATION DATA
Cox, Jeff, 1940-
    Landscape with roses / Jeff Cox ; photographs by Jerry Pavia.
       p. cm.
    ISBN 1-56158-382-0
     1. Rose culture. 2. Roses. 3. Landscape gardening. I. Title.
SB411 .C786 2002
635.9'33734--dc21   2001043371

Printed in Singapore
10 9 8 7 6 5 4 3 2 1

For Susanna, the loveliest rose in the garden.

—Jeff Cox

To my partner, Vicki Long. I am honored by her patience, her help on all my projects, and, most of all, her love.

—Jerry Pavia

Acknowledgments

I'd like to offer my heartfelt thanks to Lee Anne White, my editor, who patiently and professionally reined me in and cleaned up my prose; Anne Halpin, who helped get the book off the ground; Jerry Pavia, whose photographs bring the book to life; and the following rosarians for their assistance and suggestions: Lloyd Brace of Waldoboro, Maine; James and Eva Estes of Keller, Texas; Cindy Hattersley of Carmel, California; Gregg Lowery of Sebastopol, California; Jonathan Plant of St. Helena, California; Rayford Reddell of Petaluma, California; and Carolyn Stone of Kenwood, California.   —Jeff Cox

I would like to thank all the garden owners whose gardens are in this book. Without their generosity in sharing their gardens, usually at odd hours, there would be no garden books in bookstores. A special thanks to Ann Armstrong, Pat Henry, and Connie Cross for always sharing their gardens and leading me to many others. Thanks to Jeff Cox, the author of this book, our third together, for finding the most beautiful words to accompany my images. And a heartfelt thanks to my assistants, Jan Rose and Trish Bryant, who worked very hard to bring this book to fruition.

—Jerry Pavia

Contents

Introduction

ROSE LOVERS live in the best of times. Here in America, for the past century or so, roses have been treated as beautiful but finicky garden invalids requiring separate beds where they could be sprayed, pruned, fed, and nursed into bloom, apart from the rest of the garden and landscape, which required comparatively little maintenance. We loved them so that they were worth the effort, but a whole new world of landscaping with roses is opening up for gardeners.

I first became excited about these new possibilities in the early 1990s when I was hosting a Public Broadcasting System (PBS) television program called *Your Organic Garden*, and we visited Rayford Reddell's Garden Valley Ranch and Rose Nursery in Petaluma, California. Reddell introduced me to 'Climbing Iceberg', among other treasures, and explained how breeders were producing new strains with special qualities. A few years later, when I was hosting *Grow It!* on the Home and Garden Television Network (HGTV), Reddell introduced me to 'Carefree Delight' and other low-maintenance roses. After testing a number of these new introductions in my own garden and discovering their versatility, the idea for this book was born.

(Pat and Ron Vandenberghe garden, Danville, CA)

Recent advances in breeding have created hardier, disease-resistant, repeat-blooming, and smashingly beautiful roses. Now these most treasured plants are leaping out of old-fashioned rose gardens and consorting with shrubs and perennials in mixed beds and borders, twining their way into trees like floral halos, covering bare soil with rich colors, and adorning all sorts of architectural structures. Roses have a place in garden rooms, among foundation plantings, along the woodland edge, and in containers on patios and terraces. There are even roses that will tolerate a little shade, offer stunning fall leaf color, or produce brightly colored hips.

These new low-maintenance plants don't supplant the thousands of favorites from the late 19th and entire 20th centuries, or the beloved roses of the more distant past. Many time-honored, old-fashioned roses have been kept in commerce through the years because of their beauty and utility in adorning the home landscape. But today's new breeds of roses add to the opportunities to create landscapes filled with color and fragrance. You can choose from hundreds of new roses that combine the best of plant form, foliage, and flowers of the past with a rainbow of colors, and a wide range of fragrances. New types of roses grow well in a variety of soils and conditions, stand up to heavy rains, survive bitter winters, and produce loads of gorgeous flowers all season long—and without a lot of work on our part.

In this book, I've tried to give you innovative ideas to capitalize on this new rose versatility. As for their traditional uses, you can continue to use roses' unsurpassed ability to beautify a home and landscape by training them up walls and pillars, covering arbors and pergolas, rambling on fences and trellises, and splashing long vistas with bold drifts of color. And while you may not have used roses in the middle of a dense group of woody shrubs because of concerns about reaching them for chores like deadheading and disease control, you now have varieties that will bloom all summer without much attention.

This book is about the beauty and utility of roses that remain unrivaled by any other ornamental in the plant kingdom. It's my hope that *Landscape with Roses* will help you express your artistic virtuosity in the garden, increase the beauty of your home and property, and enhance your affection for roses—the affection that makes growing these plants such a joy.

(Ellsworth garden, Yountville, CA)

(Susan Newell garden, Rancho Santa Fe, CA)

ONE

ROSES
for any
SETTING

Designing with Roses ◍ The Diversity of Roses ◍
Roses around the House ◍ Roses in Mixed
Plantings ◍ Roses throughout the Landscape ◍
Roses on Structures

Chapter 1

Designing with Roses

ROSES ARE THE STARS of the show. More than any other similarly sized shrubs, they become a visible part of the garden's design: its composition, heights, masses, forms, and focal points. They draw attention to themselves because of their color, like the Floribunda 'All That Jazz', with its bright, coral-salmon hue, or because of their astonishing subtle beauty, like the Shrub rose 'Sparrieshoop', with single, light pink blossoms that look like painted porcelain. And they lend drama to the landscape, especially the larger roses that can turn a simple path into a channel of color.

A lavish, *traditional English mixed border includes repetitive drifts of foxgloves and Shrub roses. A brick wall serves as the perfect backdrop.*
(Sally Cooper garden, Charlotte, NC; preceding pages: Carol Brewer garden, El Cajon, CA)

The boxwood hedges direct foot traffic around a tableau featuring two of David Austin's English roses—the medium red 'Wenlock' (left) and light pink 'Tamora' (right)—and an armillary sundial. *(Sabrina and Freeland Tanner garden, Napa Valley, CA)*

It is traditional to place the formal beds closest to the house, the semiformal ones beyond them, and the informal landscaping at a farther distance still.

Suitable for Any Style Garden

You can use the knowledge of roses' dramatic appearance in formal, semi-formal, and informal ways. A landscape may be exclusively one of these styles, or it may be a mix of the three. If a landscape is to range from formal to informal, it is traditional to place the formal beds closest to the house, the semiformal ones beyond them, and the informal landscaping at a farther distance still—the implication being that beyond the informal landscape is the wild wood (even though it may just be the neighbor's yard). That's the traditional way, but it's entirely possible to surround part of the house with informal areas or semiformal beds and reserve an outlying spot for a formal garden. Whatever makes sense and pleases you provides your guiding star in landscape design.

Fancying the Formal

In ages past, when nature was mostly beyond human control, a tight order was the goal of garden design. Cloistered gardens, formal parterres, and meticulously manicured gardens were the rage. Nature was brushed aside, and the landscape was bent to purely human ideas. Clipped hedges, arabesques of herbs and boxwood, rows of roses flanking paths, formal fountains and water features—these suggested that humans were in complete control. Plants provided the textures and colors for replicating a fancy tapestry or brocade. One could easily make sense out of such a landscape, and it gave those for whom nature was still a chaotic and dangerous place a sense of order and security.

Even though they can be the most elaborate of designs, and despite changes in attitude toward formal gardens, they are still the most obvious way to display roses in massed plantings. This is especially true in large, expansive landscapes where the patterns of large, formal plantings can be seen in their entirety. The formal rose garden will have its season of major bloom, and then rebloomers will produce flowers sporadically throughout the remainder of the season. Formal gardens can be kept in color by planting bulbs and annuals among the roses. Early bulbs flower in spring, along with the roses, and once the roses have begun to leaf out, annuals can be added for summer color. Flowering ground covers and low-growing perennials are also good choices

A very happy specimen of the Bourbon rose *'Zéphirine Drouhin' softens the stone wall of this European home.* (Nathalie Becq garden, Grisy, France)

The keys to a well-designed formal garden are geometry, symmetry, and repetition.

A formal garden *combines symmetry and repetition. The severe lines of this example are softened by the charming and fragrant white Noisette 'Mme. Alfred Carrière'.* (Ray Reddell garden, Petaluma, CA)

for adding a splash of color through the season. Just remember to choose flowering plants that harmonize with the color of any reblooming roses in your garden.

The keys to a well-designed formal garden are geometry, symmetry, and repetition—repetition of form, color, and design, front to back and top to bottom. Find a simple, pleasing design that includes roses and just one or two other elements—such as under-planted ground covers and chipped gravel paths—repeat it throughout, and you will have a formal garden. Then add statuary, or perhaps a sundial, as a focal point at the center of a circle or arc, or at the end of a straight path to draw your eye.

A Garden Just for Roses

Since showy roses demand attention and clamor for center stage, why not give it to them? There will always be a cherished spot for the formal rose garden—even though there are a multitude of other uses for roses in today's landscape. In addition, you may choose to set aside a garden for cutting or a garden for your collection of roses.

A Simple Garden Plan

To create a formal garden, you need a formal, geometric design such as this one, featuring circles within a square. Start by drawing an 18-inch square on a large sheet of paper. Determine the center of the square by drawing diagonal lines from the corners. Then, using a compass placed at the center point where the lines cross, draw a circle that touches each side of the square. This circle will have a 9-inch radius. Draw a second circle with a 7-inch radius. The space between these circles is a 2-foot path. Now, quarter the center circle by drawing diagonals from the corners of the square to the opposite corner. Measure 1 inch on either side of the diagonal and draw lines parallel to it, but only in the center circle. This quarters the center circle with 2-foot-wide paths that cross in the center.

To transfer these measurements to the garden, convert inches to feet to create an 18-foot-square garden.

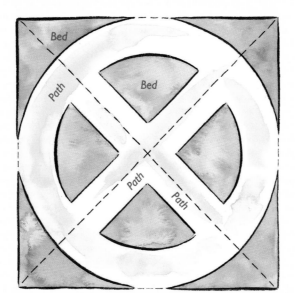

This formal garden plan is a simple design with paths and geometric planting beds.

Use a string with a center stake or nail as a compass, and flour or lime as a marker. Follow the same steps as drawing your design on paper.

Limit Plant Selection

Such formal arrangements are often most effective if planted entirely with the same rose or several distinct groupings of roses. This will give it a solid look, with shrubs of the same height and color. Another option is to select several roses with differently colored flowers but similar height. In any case, limit the types and colors of roses you choose.

This garden has eight planting spaces: four pie-shaped wedges in the center circle and four corner sections outside a circular path, creating a generous 200 square feet for your roses, all in a compact 18-foot square. For variety, consider planting three small (18 to 24 inches) roses in each corner wedge, and three medium (36 to 40 inches) roses in each quarter of the circle for a total of 24 roses, without crowding.

Allow each plant enough room to receive plenty of sunlight on its sides so that it can flower over its entire surface, not just at the growing tips. To add a finishing touch, anchor your rose garden with a formal element like a fountain, statue, or even an old-fashioned Victorian gazing ball in the center.

A semiformal garden has looser plantings and softer edges but still retains a strong sense of design and order. The Hybrid Perpetual 'Arrillaga' anchors this passage.

Peaceful, Semiformal Settings

In a semiformal garden, beds may be formal or geometric in design, but with loose, informal plantings—as opposed to those that are clipped and highly manicured. More often, however, the borders in a semiformal garden are curved, and island beds tend to be oblong or free-form in shape. The curves are easy and gentle, giving the landscape a peaceful, restful look. Lawn plays a significant role in the semiformal garden. Even though it may not form the largest part of the landscape, still it is there, like a rug on which the furniture sits. The lawn ties all the parts together—the beds, borders, pathways, arches, water features—and in most gardens, transforms into pathways down which people meander.

The semiformal rose garden may have some formal elements admixed with more free-form ones. For instance, there may be a set of stone steps, benches, pillars, or urns, but they are set amid a more relaxed grouping of planting areas. Statuary appears not at strict focal points or at the ends of pathways, but set back in the shrubbery a bit or off to one side of a path. Discoveries become possible in the semiformal landscape as grassy alleys lead you into graceful turns around tall hedges or planting beds into new garden areas.

Pleasant balance, versus symmetry, is the key to the semiformal rose garden. Plants can mix and tumble together naturally, but you will have planned their placement carefully to achieve a satisfying composition. Repetition is still important in the semiformal rose garden, but the rhythm of the repetition is more syncopated: A group of the same roses is not planted exactly every 15 feet down the edge of the path, but groups of varying numbers of roses are mixed into the bed or border farther apart or closer together, depending on how the composition balances. A small group of very dark-foliaged, deep-red roses might be balanced by a

The beds are laid out *formally, but the plantings within them are loose and lush, creating a semiformal style. The red Hybrid Tea 'Guy Laroche' is on the left. The white rose on the right is the Climbing Tea 'Sombreuil'. (Sabrina and Freeland Tanner garden, Yountville, CA)*

A Quick, Easy Pillar

Cut and roll a section of concrete-reinforcing wire mesh into a circular cage—18 to 24 inches in diameter and as tall as you wish—to make an open pillar for Climbing roses. To hold the cylinder together, slip the cut ends of wire through the mesh squares and use pliers to bend them back. Secure the bottom of the cylinder firmly into the ground with aluminum tent pegs or similar stakes. Next, plant a Climbing rose whose mature size is slighting taller than hat of the pillar on either side the cage, wind their canes in opposite directions, and tie them loosely with twine. Finally, plant some colorful annuals or long-blooming perennials at the base of the pillar to hide the stakes.

Create a rose pillar from a section of concrete-reinforcing wire mesh that is rolled and then pegged in the ground.

One easy way to give your garden an informal look is to let a few roses grow as they will, without much pruning.

larger planting of light pink, frothy roses; heavy, dark areas of flower or foliage have more visual weight than airy, open, and light-colored plants. Neatness still rules in a semiformal garden, with manicured lawns, edged beds, and well-behaved plantings, but there is not as great a sense of control as there might be in a formal garden.

Playfulness and a Touch of Informality

With informal design, we move away from neatly arranged beds and borders—not toward chaos, but toward a more easygoing style. If there are architecture elements—such as steps, balconies, or fences—they serve as scaffolding for roses rather than focal points. Roses can be encouraged to grow up into existing trees and shrubs. And if there are large expanses of lawn or meadow, roses can be planted en masse or scattered about randomly among the wildflowers. Nature, however, has rhyme and reason, and anarchy is no substitute for an informal design: Even our informal landscapes, lush with roses, need an informed hand to guide them.

An informal design is relaxed. Rambling and climbing roses contribute to this feeling, whether they grow on fences and arbors or into trees. Pillars and pergolas bring formality to the scene, so avoid them if informality is your aim. Be playful. Bright colors against wood or tile, broken crockery and dishes set into a walkway, or perhaps sculptures or ornaments tucked in among carefree roses help create an informal, fun atmosphere.

Informal means blurring the edges a bit. If you have a woodland area or a cluster of tall trees, plant a few tall foliage shrubs such as laurustinus (*Viburnum tinus*), *Euonymus*, and privet (*Ligustrum* spp.) among them. Then tuck a shade-tolerant landscape rose just behind one of the tall shrubs so it's peeking out, and another one or two toward the front. Use several groupings of perennials—not just flowering perennials, but also foliage plants like *Rodgersia*, *Hosta*, variegated ivy (*Hedera helix* cvs.), bear's breeches (*Acanthus mollis*), and ornamental grasses like *Miscanthus*, *Carex*, and *Pennisetum* species—near the roses. If the area is large enough, include a pathway for exploring the garden further.

One easy way to give your garden an informal look is to let a few roses grow as they will, without much pruning. I've seen the Kordes rose 'Erfurt' handled this way—whether by design or neglect I'm not sure, but the neglect in this case was benign. 'Erfurt' made a mounding shrub

A wrought-iron arbor *adds some structure to a lush and casual planting. The Modern Climber 'America' is beginning to clamber up the arbor, while the white-and-pink Hybrid Tea 'Grace de Mónaco' watches on the right.*

about 5 feet tall, densely branched, with green foliage washed with coppery overtones, and gorgeous, single, cherry-pink flowers fading to white in the center, where a puff of golden stamens added to a jeweled look.

In an informal garden, simple is better than complex; and ironically, the very informality of an arrangement often results in a hard-to-read complexity. I remember admiring a landscape where the homeowners had simply trucked in soil to make a gentle hillock about 30 feet across and 6 feet high in their front yard. It was planted with low-growing grasses and slender birches. From the street you could look through the birches to a group of tall roses—they may have been on some form of support, but I couldn't see it—flecking the background with color. It was simple, with just the elements of grassy hillock, birches, and roses. But it was both enormously inviting and very effective.

Design Inspiration

Much of our approach to designing gardens and placing roses within them comes from other cultures. After all, roses have been cherished and cultivated for centuries, and they were first brought to America by settlers from European countries. But new garden styles are emerging too, and many of them are coming from American designers. In designing our home landscapes, we can draw inspiration from these various styles, recall memories of favorite gardens visited, or create innovative gardens that reflect our own interests and personalities.

A Rich British Heritage

The English are very much informed by the 19th-century plantsman William Robinson, and his friend Gertrude Jekyll. Both were extremely influential in putting an end to the formal Victorian garden, with its topiaries and parterres, and inventing new approaches to placing plants in the landscape, many of which are still used today. Robinson invited roses into the garden and encouraged their under-planting with fine-leaved and small-flowered perennials like pinks (*Dianthus* spp.), basket of gold (*Aurinia saxatilis*), Irish moss (*Soleirolia soleirolii*), violets (*Viola* spp.),

Suit Your Style

Roses that bloom on old wood and need pruning only for occasional shaping and the removal of old, crowded stems are the best choices for an informal setting. Good examples are the Albas, Gallicas, Damasks, Centifolias, and Moss roses. In a more austere or classic setting, a Hybrid Tea that takes hard pruning during the dormant season and summer pruning to maintain shape and encourage repeat flowering might work best.

A rustic cabin demands an informal garden. This garden includes the Austin rose 'L. D. Braithwaite' along with spires of foxglove (**Digitalis purpurea**) and a fluttering covey of yellow columbines (**Aquilegia spp.**). (Kathy Whiteside garden, Madison, GA)

low-growing forms of bellflowers (*Campanula* spp.), primroses (*Primula* spp.), coral bells (*Heuchera* spp.), and many varieties of stonecrop (*Sedum* spp.). Jekyll grew other plants beneath her Shrub roses, and was especially fond of the silver-leaved lambs' ears (*Stachys byzantina*) and catmint (*Nepeta* spp.). But her chief contribution was to suggest that the way to put a garden together was to plan out the architectural elements—the paths, walls, fences, and arbors—and then use roses and perennials to interrupt straight lines and soften hard edges.

The classic modern English garden, which is semiformal in nature, can perhaps best be seen at Sissinghurst, in Kent, England, where plantswoman Vita Sackville-West created "a tumble of roses and honeysuckle, figs and vines"—and, she might have added, foxgloves. While she primarily worked with once-blooming old roses, her beloved Sissinghurst is now replete with continuous bloomers that carry her ideas of lush glory throughout the entire growing season.

From England, we also have the cottage garden—that quaint home with lots of colorful flowers out front. While these modest front-yard gardens were often quite structured, with straight paths leading to the doorway and axial paths as well, they were generally planted very loosely,

Climbers and Shrub roses *add charm and romance to a cottage's walls, attached arbor, and porch. The Climbing Tea 'Sombreuil' graces the wall, while a very floriferous 'Blush Noisette' climbs the porch post. The Floribunda 'Escapade' chimes in with pink blooms in the planting bed below.* (Joy Wolff garden, Healdsburg, CA)

often haphazardly, with a profusion of herbs, vegetables, and old-fashioned flowers. Roses, with their bright colors and abundant flowers, are very much at home in the cottage garden.

Several roses are perfectly at home in this Mediterranean-style garden whose strongest visual element is the almost black succulent Aeonium arboreum 'Zwartkop'. (Valentine Garden designed by Isabelle Green, Santa Barbara, CA)

Of French and Italian Descent

Despite the formality of Versailles, most French gardens are informal in style. They are floriferous, with roses serving as backdrops for lots of variously colored perennials and shrubs. This is a generalization, of course—northern France is very different from the Côte d'Azur, Brittany from Savoie in the foothills of the Alps, and the forests of the Massif Central from them all. But there is a certain Gallic sensibility that ties them together, and it has to do with the passionate love the French have for the landscape and the romance of plants. So, although precision may have been a hallmark of early French estate gardens, it is more common for the French to throw order out the window, and to fill their properties with flowers.

Contrast Flower Size

Small-flowered roses like Miniatures and Polyanthas get an extra visual kick when accompanied by large-flowered plants like clematis and hydrangea. Contrast large-flowered roses with small-flowered plants like baby's breath (*Gypsophila paniculata*) and candytuft (*Iberis sempervirens*).

Throughout Italy, roses are used extensively both to cover ancient buildings and add bright splashes of color to gardens filled with Mediterranean herbs.

A pretty lantern *very effectively emerges from behind the sumptuous pink Austin Shrub rose 'Emanuel' and blue* **Anchusa. Sprays of the yellow Austin 'Graham Thomas' are on the right.** *(Sabrina and Freeland Tanner garden, Yountville, CA)*

European Accents

Visitors to European gardens, especially those in Mediterranean countries, often return home enthused to re-create the look of, say, a garden they saw in Italy. This is easier to accomplish in California, with its Mediterranean climate, than in the woods of Virginia. But it's not impossible for a Virginian to use a Tuscan concept to plan a landscape with a fountain, herb and flower beds backed by tall yews and conical junipers, and perhaps a potting shed plastered and washed in a sunny ochre with the arching stems of an 'Old Pink Moss' rose trained up one wall. The secret is choosing varieties of plants that will adapt to the climate and using hardscaping elements that look good in a variety of settings.

The Italian gardens of antiquity were very formal, often with elaborate water features. The rectangular pools of water are still seen in modern Italian gardens, but the elaborate fountains are much less common. Due to the hot Mediterranean climate and sparse summer rain in central to southern Italy, flower gardens tend to be small and close to buildings. Roses are used extensively both to cover the ancient buildings and add bright splashes of color to gardens filled with Mediterranean herbs.

Arbors and pergolas offer shade from the relentless sun, and are often draped in grape vines or Climbing roses. In the north, gardens tend to be lush and woodsy. Garden rooms are enclosed by coniferous walls. Orchards, vineyards, and roses seem to go together there.

Why Climate Makes Such a Difference

As the United States is the melting pot of the world, so its gardens represent just about all types of designs from other countries. The limiting factor, however, is climate. In the warm, well-watered coastal areas of the Pacific Northwest, as well as other regions in USDA Hardiness Zones 6 to 9 that receive ample rainfall, a wide range of roses and perennials can be grown, and lush mixed borders are common. Because irrigation isn't a necessity, roses can also romp through the landscape. Across the Sunbelt, roses proliferate in the hot, moist climate. The Cherokee rose (*R. laevigata*), a single rose that grows to 15 feet with a huge, bushy habit, has, along with its cultivars, been planted in southern gardens for more than 200 years. It has also escaped to the wild, and its position in the natural landscape can tell you a lot about where to site roses in your southern landscape to good effect.

In the cold, northern tier of states, a smaller palette of roses and other perennials is available and most of these hardy roses tend to be once-bloomers. This limits their use in beds and borders where continuous bloom is often the goal, so gardeners in North Dakota, Minnesota, Montana, and other northern states more often use roses to dress up fences, walls, and arbors. By contrast, growers in California's 300-plus-day-growing-season regions have almost the entire family of roses to choose. Yet, water is scarce and irrigation is a must—so all ornamental plantings tend to be concentrated and close to the home for efficiency. As a result, you'll find roses packed in mixed plantings, adorning walls, and decorating decks and patios.

In the Great Plains, winter thaws and freezes are hard on roses. This calls for growing only the toughest varieties and giving them plenty of winter protection. And in the hot, dry Southwest, one must choose roses carefully and give them a protected spot where they can receive adequate water.

In the hot, dry Southwest, one must choose roses carefully and give them a protected spot where they can receive adequate water.

When making a color combination with a strong red rose like this Floribunda 'Europeana', you can't go wrong with the silvery white foliage of dusty miller (Senecio cineraria).

> *Roses can be used in subtle ways — in simple, refined, and sophisticated landscapes that reflect a regional sense of place.*

A well-designed arbor holds the Modern Climbing rose 'America' in this tropical-looking Sunbelt garden. Flowering flax (Linum grandiflorum 'Rubrum'), California poppies (Eschscholzia californica), and borage (Borago officinalis) flank the path from left to right in the foreground.
(Pat Welsh garden, Del Mar, CA)

Toward an American Style

Is there an American style? Not really. Americans have adopted all styles, from the lush, Spanish-style gardens of southern California to the English beds and borders on Long Island to the tropical gardens of Hawaii. Yet, two distinctly American styles seem to be emerging. One style is to spotlight hot-colored annuals and tender perennials among masses of large-leaved foliage plants—a style dubbed by some as "tropicalismo." This often means associating roses with broad-leaved, tropical-looking companions. In the gardens of moderate climates, this could include Adam's needle (*Yucca filamentosa*) and Japanese aralia (*Fatsia japonica*). In containers, there are even more choices: Among them are tender, semitropical and tropical plants that you can overwinter indoors, such as *Canna* hybrids, elephant's ears (*Alocasia* spp.), and bananas (*Musa* spp.). Big, blowsy ornamental grasses are often added for contrast.

The other, more widely embraced style is to use roses in subtle ways—in simple, refined, and sophisticated landscapes that reflect a regional sense of place. These gardens tend to be less formal in their design, and they are especially suited to homes typical of a region. Just as homes are most often built from locally available materials—red brick in the South, wood in New England, adobe in the Southwest, or stucco in Florida—gardens are landscaped with similar materials. Painted pickets are common up and down the East Coast, split rail fences have their home in the Midwest, and cedar decks proliferate on the West Coast. Similarly, many, though certainly not all, of the plants used in these gardens are either native or naturalized in that region.

A Naturalistic Approach to Design

Nature is replete with ecologically balanced plant communities that give each area of the country a certain look. The naturalistic landscape—that which draws its inspiration from and attempts to mimic nature—is easier to plant and maintain if it incorporates features of the wilderness that existed before Columbus; that is, native plants in naturalistic habitats. It doesn't have to consist exclusively of native plants, but the plants should be arranged as they would in nature—perhaps in the layers found along the woodland edge, or in the low, mixed plantings of a prairie. If the primeval landscape was a rich mix of meadows, ponds, and coniferous woodlands moist and emerald green with moss, as one finds in northern New England, a naturalistic landscape might include a pond edged with hardy roses and blueberries, with mossy logs amid the shrubs that form the backdrop for the roses.

'Climbing Cécile Brünner', a climbing Polyantha, finds its way into the welcoming arms of an old fruit tree in a garden that gives the feeling of an old farm or homestead. (Helie Robertson garden, San Anselmo, CA)

In naturalistic-style gardens, plants should be arranged as they would grow in nature.

Roses for the Naturalistic Landscape

In nature, rose colors tend to be variations on a theme rather than confettilike splashes of dissimilar colors. So in a naturalistic landscape, pick a color, such as apple-blossom pink, and plant several low-maintenance roses with similarly colored flowers. Wild rose look-alikes such as the Multiflora 'Francis E. Lester' and Luther Burbank's 'Apple Blossom' are good candidates for this particular color theme, along with natives like the Carolina rose (*R. carolina*), *R. virginiana*, and *R. californica*.

Notice how the deep, rich red of the Hybrid Tea 'Ingrid Bergman' stands out against the strong, contrasting yellow of Scotch broom **(Cytisus scoparius).** (Joann Romano garden, San Diego, CA)

In the naturalistic rose garden, plants aren't sheared into hedges or pruned into meatballs. Instead, they are allowed to grow naturally. Likewise, lines aren't straight, and when curved, aren't regular. Pathways are not paved, but are more likely to be covered in mulch, or a mown strip through a meadow. Architectural elements, if included at all, tend to be rustic and of minor significance. Colors are used with restraint. Instead of pathways lined with evenly spaced plants, drifts of roses or other plants may flow across the path—perhaps in a group of seven shrubs, three on one side and four on the other. A naturalistic landscape is the least formal of all informal landscapes.

Applying Lessons from Nature

Getting out into the natural world, away from the cities and towns, usually allows a person to produce plenty of landscaping ideas. A landscape designer recently told me about driving through the high meadows of the Sierra Nevada Mountains. "I saw the western wild rose, a California native, growing here and there in clumps," he said. That gave him the idea of using them so they seem part of a plant community, such as the conifers, low shrubs, and grasses one sees in the high Sierra.

Find themes for your home landscape by appreciating and studying nearby native habitats. What ecological role do roses play in the wild? What functions has nature endowed them with? How will they add to the backyard community's health and diversity? Having answers to these questions will allow us to develop landscapes that are more than just decorative. A beautiful wild landscape is a working environment for the community of creatures that inhabit that territory—both plants and animals. Home landscaping ideas based on what works in the wild therefore work with nature's forces, not against them.

Roses are essentially woody shrubs, so use them as nature uses woody shrubs—to create a dense brush, or the edging between a grassy area and taller trees. Roses like sun and adequate water, and they usually have thorns, so that suggests they evolved in areas of the world with at

Take Note of Nature

Take a notebook with you on nature walks or hikes into the woods or wild areas, or even into parks if that's what is close at hand. Look for sights that strike you as beautiful, and ask yourself why you are drawn to them. After a bit of analysis, you can jot down or sketch the features of the site in your notebook. Back home, those notes can be used to inspire an idea for your garden based on your own, personal perception of beauty as drawn from nature. You might reproduce what you've seen in the wild exactly as you saw it, miniaturize it, or create a garden that, in some simple way, evokes what you loved about the scene.

'Old Blush', *a China rose with long, slender stems and a loose, open habit, finds a partner in an opportunistic wild black cherry (Prunus serotina) in an informal spot of an Eastern landscape.*

Grow roses that arch and then tumble between large rocks on a slope.

least adequate rainfall in sunny meadows subject to grazing by large mammals. (I can personally attest to the fondness deer have for roses, thorns or not.)

Grow roses that arch and then tumble between large rocks. Think about how birds might eat rose hips and seed a property with roses under their flyways to and from the shelter of trees. Grow Climbing roses to scramble up small trees. Border walks with groupings of rose shrubs so they'll be marked in the winter by the twiggy, upright rose canes, and you'll know where to shovel the snow.

Create Garden Vignettes

Remember that roses look their best in settings, just as jewels do—and for the same reasons. Gregg Lowery, a nurseryman who sells vintage roses, believes "the best gardens are those in which roses play an important, but not *the* most important, role." A single rose bush or small group of three calls attention to its details. A dozen massed roses makes a strong impression, especially from a distance, but the details are lost.

Using roses in ways other than massed also forces you to think about what to plant with them. Consider plants that will go in front of roses, such as the tossing sprays of ornamental grasses or the attractive blue flowers of Russian sage (*Perovskia atriplicifolia*), blue mist shrub (*Caryopteris* × *clandonensis* 'Blue Mist'), speedwell (*Veronica* spp.), or lavender (*Lavandula* spp.). Choose from among annuals, bulbs, and perennials, and select varieties with well-behaved growth habits. Rangy plants and aggressive spreaders are generally poor choices for mixed plantings.

Just like the perennials in front of them, roses need backdrops. Buildings, particularly when coordinated with flower color, make excellent backdrops, as do walls and fences. What could be lovelier than a white picket fence draped in colorful, fragrant, deep red roses? Hedges, especially dark, evergreen hedges, may be the ideal backdrops for roses; just remember to leave room between the hedges and the roses for hedge-trimming and rose-pruning duties. Evergreen trees, especially dwarf conifers, also make handsome pair-

Avoid silhouetting roses on a ridgeline; when backlit, you can't see their gorgeous flowers very well, and any coarse foliage or awkwardness of shape is accentuated.

It was from the continuous blooming habit of China roses, such as 'Old Blush' here paired with Nepeta 'Six Hills Giant', that most of today's Modern roses acquired their everblooming abilities. (*Chris Spindler garden, Calverton, NY*)

ings. Avoid silhouetting roses on a ridgeline; when backlit, you can't see their gorgeous flowers very well, and any coarse foliage or awkwardness of shape is accentuated.

Roses Complement Any Color Scheme

Roses come in just about every flower color except purple and violet. This gives you a huge selection of colors to use in the garden—from hot, tropical tangerines to cool, somber mauves; from bright whites and light yellows to reds so dark they look almost black; and from the most saturated and intense colors to the faintest pastels.

Our reaction to colors can be personal. A certain hue of creamy orange-red might make me think of my childhood lunches and all those bowls of cream of tomato soup I stared at while eating my grilled-cheese sandwiches. And the reaction can be emotional, as when the combination of dark violet and green gives me a sick feeling in the pit of my stomach, or when vermilion and bright blue-green together make me feel happy. We can use these ideas when selecting colors for the garden, especially rose colors, to evoke very personal and emotional responses in ourselves.

While color in the garden isn't quite the same as color in a painting—for colors in a garden are constantly changing with the quality and quantity of light—most agree that red, yellow, and orange are warm colors, and that green, blue, and violet are cool colors. The hot colors we hear a lot about in gardening circles these days are simply heavily saturated (almost electric) colors. Pastels, on the other hand, are soft and light, but not pale or washed out. And while white, black, and silver aren't really colors, we can't talk color without them. By understanding these colors and how they are perceived, we can create mood in the garden.

A peaceful mood is created by the pastel pink flowers of the Modern Shrub 'Fritz Nobis', casually draping themselves over the arm of a weathered garden bench.

Selecting Your Favorite Rose Color

A visit to an extensive rose garden in a town or city near you can be very instructive. As you look across dozens, even hundreds, of roses in bloom, you can decide which colors please you most. Take along a slender book of paint samples or color swatches for comparison so you don't forget the exact color you've chosen as your favorite. Let this color anchor your garden compositions. You can always carry along the color chip when shopping for plants.

Attracting Attention

The brightest colors in the garden are the warm colors—those cherry reds, clear yellows, and vivid oranges. They are visually exciting and convey a sense of energy. When you look at a garden, plants with these colors in their flowers and foliage will be the first to catch your eye. They will almost seem to jump out at you. And when visiting a nursery or thumbing through a color catalog, they will call attention to themselves. It is tempting to take home only those roses that sound the loudest siren, but these colors should be used thoughtfully and with restraint.

In a broad landscape, distant masses of brightly colored roses can be striking. Yet in a smaller garden, bright masses can be overwhelming or distracting. But even this can be used to advantage. If you want to screen

Bright colors—cherry reds, clear yellows, and vivid oranges—are visually exciting and convey a sense of energy.

Color itself can become a focal point. The eye falls first on the bright red color of 'Blaze', a popular R. wichurana *hybrid, before it moves to the right to enjoy the pale pink blossoms of 'Jayne Austin'.* (Fred Bettin and Dean Ickes garden, Charlotte, NC)

In a smaller garden, bright masses can be overwhelming and distracting.

off a swimming pool, for instance, try planting a hedge of brightly colored roses. Not only will you create a physical barrier, the colorful flowers (when in bloom) will command so much attention that you won't see anything except the roses.

Perhaps the best use of bright colors is as an accent, or focal point. Just a few red, orange, or yellow roses will liven up a planting of softer colors. You can also create a color scheme around a hot color, even though you may use that color sparingly. For instance, light pinks and salmons key off red, while apricots and pale yellows go well with a rich yellow or orange. In general, place the stronger colors lower in the garden, near ground level, and the softer colors higher—perhaps even along a fence or wall, or climbing up a pillar or arbor.

Cool colors are just the opposite of warm colors. They recede into a garden, helping to create a sense of depth. Blue, violet, and green are typically the last colors you see in a garden. In fact, think about it: Green is the most predominant color in any garden, yet it's often the last one we notice, if we notice it at all. There aren't many cool-colored roses, but blue and violet flowers generally make wonderful companions for roses.

Eye-Pleasing Pastels

Lavender, peach, salmon, pink, and soft yellow are pastel colors. While soft, they are also bright, so they will draw your eye. Yet, unlike warm colors, they are not so strong that they don't allow your eye to move easily around the garden. In very bright light, pastels can appear washed out unless they are placed on a dark background. So if you're working in full sun, consider planting pastel roses against a backdrop of dark-green conifers rather than a white wall or fence for best effect.

Of all the rose colors, pastels are the easiest to work with and, many would agree, the most pleasing to the eye (even if they're not your favorite colors). They tend to soften the bolder colors in a garden composition, and mixed with other similar colors—cream with pale apricot, for instance, or shell pink with salmon—have a soft, restful effect as the colors change subtly through a bed or border. Colors can be provided entirely by roses or by a mix of roses and other flowering plants.

Consider planting pastel roses against a backdrop of dark green conifers rather than a white wall or fence for best effect.

A diminutive pairing and lovely color combination is given by 'Judy Fischer', a pink Miniature rose, and the violet and yellow flecks of Johnny jump-ups (Viola tricolor). (Fred Bettin and Dean Ickes garden, Charlotte, NC)

Harmonizing Colors

There are certain colors that create harmonious, even romantic combinations. If you are familiar with the color wheel, these are colors that are close to one another. Red, red-orange, and orange; yellow, yellow-green, and green; and blue, blue-violet, and violet are three examples of harmonious color combinations.

Strong colors can harmonize, *as shown by these three roses with hues close together on the color wheel. The colors of the bright red Floribunda 'Trumpeter' and yellow Austin 'Golden Celebration' mingle in the brassy apricot hue of Floribunda 'Brass Band'.* (Ruth Meehl garden, San Diego, CA)

For a lively juxtaposition, consider pairing complementary colors. These are colors with the greatest color contrast, and which appear opposite one another on the color wheel. Examples include red and green, violet and yellow, and blue and orange. Placing these colors together will stimulate your senses. For a more pleasing effect, you might consider using one color as your primary color and the other as an occasional accent. A sea of violet or lavender flowers simply begs for a yellow rose bush.

The Color Blenders

Because white is neutral, it combines well with any other color. It's especially effective against a dark background, such as tall shrubs and understory trees set in shade, with the white roses displayed in a sunny area just forward of the shady area. White roses are often used to separate areas with different color schemes—for instance, an area devoted to yellow, apricot, and pale orange flowers can be separated

White, given by the Floribunda 'Iceberg' (background) and petunias (middle), adds freshness and helps blend bright colors into a harmonious whole.

by white roses from an area of pink and deep blue flowers. White roses also work well with other white flowers and with foliage that has white variegations, such as *Hosta sieboldii*, variegated box elder (*Acer negundo* 'Variegatum'), Pagoda dogwood (*Cornus alternifolia* 'Argentea'), or the impossibly beautiful *Salix integra* 'Hakuronishiki'. All-white gardens can be beautiful—but they require constant deadheading to keep them looking fresh as the flowers fade.

White is also a showstopper. No matter what else you have in the garden, no matter how bright and electric the colors, white will always win. A single white flower has more drawing power than a mass of red ones—so use white intentionally, not incidentally. (See the sidebar on p. 34.)

All-white gardens can be beautiful—but they require constant deadheading to keep them looking fresh as the flowers fade.

Gray and silver, such as the silver foliage of *Artemisia* or lamb's ears (*Stachys byzantina*), are also blenders. And unlike white-flowered roses or perennials, they continue to perform their peacekeeping duties long after most flowers have faded. Silver foliage is especially soothing when mixed with pastels.

Choice Roses

with White Flowers

'Alba Semi-plena' ✿ An old European Alba, it produces a single flush of very fragrant, semidouble, pure white flowers on a shrub that can reach 8 feet if trained up. Grown naturally, it makes a mounding, 5-foot shrub. Zone 3.

'Blanc Double de Coubert' ✿ A Hybrid Rugosa with fragrant, double, snow-white flowers with a clutch of golden stamens in the center. It grows 4 feet tall and wide and is a star performer in the mixed border. Zone 3.

'Frau Karl Druschki' ✿ A Hybrid Perpetual that makes a 7-foot shrub with a big flush of double, white flowers in June and repeats

'Iceberg'

blooms later in the season if deadheaded. It can be trained up a pillar or post. Zone 4.

'Iceberg' ✿ The choicest of all the white Floribunda roses. It has lightly fragrant, double, white flowers, grows 4 feet tall, and is disease-free. Zone 5.

'Mme. Hardy' ✿ A very old Damask with a perfumelike scent. Its frilly and quartered, old-fashioned, white flowers are perfection in form. Reaching 6 feet, it is good at the back of a border, or growing up a porch post. Zone 4.

'White Wings' ✿ A Hybrid Tea that forms a 3- to 4-foot shrub and produces 4-inch, single, white flowers with a clutch of brown stamens in the center throughout the growing season. Great for the front of the border. Zone 5.

Gray-green leaves *are especially good foils for pink and red roses. Here* **Rosa laevigata,** *the Cherokee rose, consorts with dusty miller (***Senecio viravira***).*

Climate Affects Color

Do your best to coordinate colors so you achieve a pleasing effect, but be aware that many roses show subtle color changes depending on weather conditions. A rose lover in the southeast once described to me how her David Austin Shrub rose 'Heritage' changed from its usual clear pink to a pale, pinkish-ivory color, and wondered whether the change could be due to the extremely hot, humid weather her region had experienced during the spring. It certainly could be, as rose color is indeed weather-related. Some growers report that 'Heritage' is never a clear pink for them, but rather a pearlescent pink, and during very hot weather, it turns apricot. 'Sunset Celebration' is a relatively new rose that changes subtly depending on location. Blossoms may be apricot burnished with cream, amber-orange blushed with pink, or some other variation.

Favorite Rose Combinations

When putting different varieties of roses close to each other, be sure to coordinate their colors. You'll discover your own favorite partners, but here are a few of my favorites:

- Creamy-white 'Sombreuil' with cherry-pink 'Parade'
- Bluish-white 'Moonstone' with dark pink 'Rina Hugo'
- White 'Iceberg' with strong red 'Europeana'
- Orange 'Fragrant Cloud' with yellow 'Elina'
- Deep red 'Mr. Lincoln' with pink-and-yellow 'Peace'
- Lavender 'Angel Face' and orange 'Brandy'
- Peach 'Abbaye de Cluny' with deep pink 'Yves Piaget', under-planted with warm, pale pink 'Souvenir de la Malmaison' and shell-pink 'Gruss an Aachen'
- Bright orange blend 'Perfect Moment' with yellow blend 'St. Patrick'
- Gray-lavender 'Stainless Steel' with orangey-red 'Dolly Parton'

'The Fairy', a deservedly popular Polyantha, shows the value in planting several of the same kind of rose when creating a low hedge to mark a property boundary.

To some extent, especially with the lighter pastels, rose color is related to temperature conditions as the bud is developing. Some roses actually range from pink to yellow. But these color reactions aren't permanent, and when grown under typical weather conditions, most roses show the colors for which they are known. From region to region, differences in climate, soil, elevation, slope direction, and drainage can affect the color and shape of a rose. Roses show regional variations in size and color, just as cabernet sauvignon grapes produce a slightly different wine everywhere they are planted, and trees exposed to strong, constant winds may grow only a third the size of the same trees grown in sheltered spots.

Achieving a Long Season of Bloom

I remember with fondness the way 'Rose de Rescht', a Portland, bloomed early in the season, and, with deadheading, came back to bloom again late in the season in an extensive garden near the building where I worked in Pennsylvania. I walked past it every day, and it was with a sad sigh that I said good-bye to its last roses in early November.

This garden had roses blooming all season, and I realized that the gardener had developed three ways to ensure this. First, she planted separate groups of three once-blooming roses. They opened sequentially, from early bloomers in May to late bloomers in July, so these groups were in flower for quite a long time. But I noticed she also had several groups of continuous bloomers to keep flowers coming right through the summer until fall. Finally, there were two places where once-bloomers and continuous bloomers were planted together. At least, this is how her strategy looked to me as I walked past her lovely garden each day, though some of the roses that opened late may have been rebloomers rather than the last flushes of continuous bloomers.

Stagger Bloom Times

Over the years, this garden has given me ideas for my own rose plantings. Even if we love the once bloomers, there's no reason to have the landscape devoid of roses in any season. In the temperate regions of the United States, May sees the opening of some wild rose varieties like *R. xanthina* f. *hugonis* and the Scots rose (*R. pimpinellifolia*), Shrub roses like 'Nevada', and early Climbers like 'Gloire de Dijon'. In early June, of course, roses come bursting out all over, with Old Garden roses, once-blooming shrubs, most Climbers, other wild species, and Ground Cover roses in full bloom. By late June, native American species, Miniatures, Floribundas, and Polyanthas bloom, while some early repeat bloomers enjoy a second flush. In mid-June or early July, depending on whether you're north or south of Zone 6, Hybrid Teas, Ramblers like 'Dorothy Perkins', and Ground Covers like 'The Fairy' come into bloom.

The Austin rose 'Heritage' *is subtly tinted in all cases, but like many roses will vary its shade depending on location, soil, and climatic conditions.*

Beautiful Foliage

Rose foliage often gets a bad reputation, and many varieties can indeed be scruffy and unattractive. But the condition of rose foliage is more often an indication of a rose's overall health and how well it's been pruned—bad foliage is often just a result of bad pruning. For example, when Modern roses like Hybrid Teas, Floribundas, and Grandifloras are deadheaded, their canes should be reduced by a third (cutting back to a five-leaflet leaf). Often, however, they are only tipped, and tipping simply produces elongated shoots that become top-heavy, flop over, and bury lower foliage in moist shade where mildew and fungus can take hold. Rose type also determines how well foliage is displayed. Rugosa hybrids usually present beautiful foliage, and David Austin's English roses were bred for compactness, which creates attractive, dense foliage.

'Maytime'

'Rose de Rescht' *is a repeat-blooming Portland that needs a hard pruning every four or five years to remain so.*

Choice Roses

for a Long Season of Bloom

'Betty Boop' 🌒 An ideal Floribunda for the landscape, with flowers and foliage from top to bottom. The semi-double, 4-inch blooms are light yellow edged in red, with sweet fragrance. A 1999 All-America selection. Zone 6.

'Cécile Brünner' 🌒 Our old friend, the Sweetheart Rose, is a Polyantha that grows to 3 feet with loads of small, double, medium pink flowers all summer long. Zone 5.

'Danaë' 🌒 An outstanding Hybrid Musk with double, rich yellow, strongly fragrant flowers on a vigorous shrub that reaches 5 to 10 feet. Can be trained as a climber. Zone 5.

'Flower Carpet' 🌒 A Modern Shrub rose that stays low and covers itself in blooms all summer. It comes with white, pink, or apple-blossom flowers and is disease-resistant. Zone 5.

'Iceberg' 🌒 This rose has it all— fragrance; lovely double, white flowers; glossy, disease-resistant foliage (except in hot, humid climates); graceful, 4-foot canes; and a bloom season that extends from spring to the edge of winter. Zone 5.

'Love' 🌒 A fine Grandiflora that forms a loose, 3-foot shrub and bears rich red flowers with silvery reverses that recur during the summer. Zone 5.

'New Dawn' 🌒 A well-behaved Rambler, this rose bears continuous trusses of double, soft pink flowers on 12-foot,

'Touch of Class'

arching stems. It tolerates difficult conditions, including partial shade. Zone 5.

'Olympiad' 🌒 An extra-thorny Hybrid Tea that makes an impenetrable, yet gorgeous, 5-foot hedge covered with bright red, velvety, double blooms. Zone 5.

'Souvenir de la Malmaison' 🌒 A compact, 3-foot Bourbon that produces exceptionally fragrant, double, shell-pink blooms all season. It prefers a sunny, dry climate but does well anywhere. Rain won't spoil its blossoms. Zone 6.

'Touch of Class' 🌒 A classy Hybrid Tea with an upright habit and excellently formed, rich pink, double flowers showing highlights of creamy coral. Loves the dry weather in the upland southwest. Zone 5.

'Betty Boop'

Most varieties with the old China roses in their heritage—including Floribundas, Polyanthas, Hybrid Teas, and Hybrid Perpetuals—will bravely open their flowers into the icy teeth of cold October nights (or even later, depending on your climate). These plants are genetically programmed to keep blooming well into fall. It gets cold where they're from but not that cold, so they keep on blooming until a hard frost really shuts them down and freezes their canes. For protection, these roses should be cut back and mulched when a serious cold snap is forecast.

Chinas, Floribundas, Polyanthas, Hybrid Teas, and Hybrid Perpetuals will bravely open their flowers into the icy teeth of cold October nights.

Hips and Leaves Extend the Season

Although it's not often pitched as a selling point in the catalogs, roses can add good fall color to the garden, and not just because they rebloom then. Many roses have wonderful fall foliage and some also have hips (swollen, seed-bearing capsules) at the end of their stems. The best fall color combination among roses could very well be between the hips and leaves of *R. glauca* (previously *R. rubrifolia*). The hips are a rich orange-

Sculpture always creates *a point of interest in a garden and is usually most effective when integrated into a setting, such as given by the Modern Shrub rose 'Red Ribbons'.*
(American Rose Center, Shreveport, LA)

Perennials and roses *often grow into loose, naturalistic plantings as they mature. Here, the Austin rose 'Belle Story' mixes with English lavender (Lavandula angustifolia) and salvia at the lower left.*

red that makes a striking combination with the plum-colored fall foliage. It's one of the prettiest rose effects I know, and yet doesn't involve the flowers at all. Because it makes such a strong statement, plant it where it can be frequently seen. I have one by the driveway where I park my car, so it greets me when I get out, and another at the entrance to a small fenced-in orchard of apples.

Rubrifolia means red-leaved, and *glauca* means bluish-gray, bluish-white, or mauve. If you grow this rose, you'll notice that all the leaves have a gray-green to mauve hue—hence, *glauca*. Those leaves that receive full sun, however, have an interesting reddish copper tint as well—hence, *rubrifolia*. In spring, the growing shoots have a bluish tint, while the buds and new wood are a darker, purplish-copper color. The single flowers open flat, and the petals are a clear, vividly bright red-pink that fades toward white near the cluster of yellow stamens in the center.

Leaves of R. *virginiana*, a species native to the eastern United States, turn golden before dropping. Another American native, the New England shining rose (R. *nitida*) is such a fall standout it's worth planting just to see its slender, small, compound leaves turn plum red and scarlet when frosts nip at it. The western wild rose (R. *woodsii* var. *fendlerii*) is a very cold-hardy (Zone 4) native of the western states, and turns a pretty scarlet to orange color in fall. In addition, it sports large, red hips that are quite showy after the leaves fall. Being native, it's at home not only in garden borders, but also in meadows, at the woods' edge, and along a driveway or roadside.

The ferny leaves of R. *pimpinellifolia* turn coppery red in the fall, and the rose's little black hips stud the foliage with jet beads. Use it as the edge of the yard or woods with companions that give brilliant-orange or flame-red color in the fall—ornamental sumacs (*Rhus* spp.), Virginia creeper (*Parthenocissus quinquefolia*), American bittersweet (*Celastrus scandens*), and dwarf crape myrtle (*Lagerstroemia* spp.).

Besides R. *glauca* and the western wild rose, several other roses are worth growing for their ornamental fruits. 'Geranium' is a cultivated variety of R. *moyesii* from China. It's a big, rangy shrub, and although 'Gera-

Plant R. pimpinellifolia along the edge of the yard with companions that give brilliant orange or flame-red fall color to complement its black hips and coppery-red foliage.

The attractive, tomatolike hips of **Rosa rugosa** make a nutritious tea and are loved by small pets like rabbits, hamsters, and chinchillas.

Many roses *have attractive fall foliage that can range in color from yellow to orange to red. This wild rose has red stems as well.*

nium' is probably the most compact of the *R. moyesii* cultivars, it can still reach 8 feet tall, with bristly, arching stems. The flowers are geranium-red and single, with clusters of distinctive yellow stamens in their centers. These are followed by oblong, scarlet hips that dot the leafless bushes in a striking display. Another variety of *R. moyesii*, 'Sealing Wax', is named for its waxy-red, extra-large hips. The hips of *R.* × *micrugosa* are reddish orange and covered with prickles. *R. pimpinellifolia* has big, rotund, shiny, red fruits, and *R. acicularis* produces flask-shaped, apple-red fruits.

Perhaps the species that's the star performer in the hips department is *R. rugosa* and its cold-hardy, salt-tolerant hybrids, which produce ochre- and mustard-colored leaves that turn russet before they fall. One of the best *R. rugosa* hybrids for fall color is the intensely fragrant 'Roseraie de l'Haÿ', named after the famous Paris rose garden. Its wrinkly, tough, compound foliage turns a rich, bronzy yellow in autumn. It's especially good in an herb garden where its rosy, magenta flowers and colorful fall leaves add beauty to the herbs. *R. rugosa* var. *alba* has gorgeous single, white flowers, while the cultivar 'Scabrosa' has rich, mauve flowers. Both of these—along with most rugosas—have large, tomato-red hips that are sensational in the landscape, especially where people can chance upon them, such as when they're planted at the margins of the garden, in fields, along roadsides, and in other spots where their low maintenance requirements can be useful.

Plant roses with large,
tomato-red hips where
people can chance
upon them.

The scarlet hips of 'Altissimo' are eye-
catchers in fall. For a rose to produce hips,
a late summer crop of flowers must be left
on the plant rather than deadheaded.

Chapter 2

The Diversity of Roses

WITH ROSES, we are afforded a genus of garden plants with un-matched diversity in form, habit, color, fragrance, and flower shape. We can make choices among many thousands of roses as dissimilar in size as 8-inch miniatures and 40-foot Climbers, with blooms as small as dimes and as large as softballs, and with flowers in almost every color of the rainbow. They are loved for their fragrance—from the sweet, fruity scent of 'Veilchenblau' to the classic perfume of 'Kazanlik'. Most roses flower once in late spring, but others

The sparkling colors of mixed beds of perennials and roses show just what these plants can do to enliven an entranceway of earthy brick and cold gray stone. (Ruth Meehl garden, San Diego, CA)

repeat sporadically in summer or fall, and some bloom continuously throughout the entire growing season. Most sport green or grayish-green foliage, but a few have strong blue or burgundy overtones and show off bright orange or red hips in fall.

In addition, many of today's newer roses can claim greater floriferousness, increased hardiness, and improved resistance to pests and diseases. They are suited not only for rose gardens, but also for mixed plantings, as alternative ground covers, in containers, and twining up all sorts of structures. In other words, there is a rose for every gardener—no matter where they live, what their taste or style, or where they wish to grow roses on their property.

When we think of roses, we usually think of very double flowers with lots of petals. But the great diversity of roses includes some magnificent simplicities, as shown by the single Hybrid Tea 'Dainty Bess' with her silvery-pink petals and fuchsia-and-brown stamens. *(Lee and Virgil Amick garden, Lexington, SC)*

What's New in Roses

Thanks to selective breeding, domesticated plants keep changing over time. Many of these changes are called "improvements" when, really, they are nothing more than variations. For example, I'm not sure *Hibiscus syriacus* 'Aphrodite', a dark pink rose of Sharon, is an improvement over 'Minerva', which is lavender-pink but otherwise very similar. Both are lovely, but one is not an improvement over the other. When it comes to roses, however, I believe there *have* been real and important improvements over the years—in addition to the hundreds of new cultivars that are hybridized each year and count only as variations.

More Floriferous Plants

Old Garden roses can be very floriferous at the peak of their blooming season, but for the rest of the year, most are just large, leafy shrubs. The

Many of today's new
roses are suited not only
for rose gardens, but
for mixed plantings.

The Modern Climbing rose 'Red Fountain'
*begins the climb up a tree, and its like-
colored partner, the* **R.** wichurana *hybrid
'Blaze', continues the ascent into the
branches.*

Chinas and Hybrid Teas offer continuous bloom, but are less hardy and more prone to pest and disease problems. The Multifloras have the sought-after trait of producing huge clusters of tiny flowers but, as discovered when they were imported to this country as cattle hedging, their aggressive nature often makes them more pestiferous than desirable. But in these roses, and others, breeders saw opportunity.

In particular, breeders wanted to produce new hybrids with more flowers per cluster, so in the late 19th century, they took stock from the weedy Multiflora rose and hybridized it with Chinas and Hybrid Teas. The resultant crosses produced the Polyanthas, which inherited the continuous-bloom gene and bear large clusters of small flowers. In addition, they are hardy, low-maintenance roses that have proven resistant to many of the diseases that plague roses.

Floribundas originated around the time of World War I when the Danish firm of Poulsen crossed a Hybrid Tea and a Polyantha, calling the result a Hybrid Polyantha. The cross resulted in a bushy rose that produced clusters of large flowers with a strong reblooming habit, and was so different from either parent that by mid-century, this new class of useful roses was renamed Floribunda.

And, as if that weren't enough, breeders then crossed these Floribundas with yet more Hybrid Teas to produce the Grandifloras. Now they had 4- to 6-foot plants with large, plump roses of the classic semidouble or double Hybrid Tea form and the floriferousness of the Floribundas—all with a continuous-blooming habit. They are not as hardy as the Floribundas, though, needing winter protection north of Zone 7.

More recently, David Austin, an English rose breeder, has produced a series of hybrids with the sought-after characteris-

The soft, coral-orange color and large, perfectly formed, 5-inch, double blossoms of 'Artistry' show why Hybrid Teas are cherished for their exquisite beauty. This one is an All-America selection that grows on long, 18-inch stems, making it perfect for the cutting garden.

Top-Rated Roses

The American Rose Society publishes a *Handbook for Selecting Roses* that rates many of the popular varieties by giving them a score on a 10-point scale. Roses rated 8.5 or higher have attributes that make them worthy in almost any garden. Among these attributes are disease resistance, excellent flower form, outstanding color, and strong flower stems. For further information, contact The American Rose Society at www.ars.org.

Another organization, All-America Rose Selections, annually names several roses to its list of winners. These pass through two or three years of trials, where they're judged on everything from disease resistance and flower production to color and fragrance. You can view all the winners from 1940 to the present at the All-America Rose Selections web site: www.rose.org. Here are some of the recent winners:

2000—'Knock Out', a cherry-red Modern Shrub; 'Crimson Bouquet', a bright red Grandiflora; and 'Gemini', a coral-pink and cream Hybrid Tea.

1999—'Candelabra', a coral-and-orange Grandiflora; 'Kaleidoscope', a lavender-pink Landscape rose; 'Fourth of July', a red-and-white Climber; and 'Betty Boop', a pale yellow Floribunda edged in red.

1998—'Fame!', a deep pink Grandiflora; 'Opening Night', a dark red Hybrid Tea; 'First Light', a light pink Landscape rose; and 'Sunset Celebration', an apricot-cream Hybrid Tea.

1997—'Artistry', a coral-orange Hybrid Tea; 'Timeless', a deep rose-pink Hybrid Tea; and 'Scentimental', a burgundy-and-cream-striped Floribunda.

1996—'St. Patrick', a chartreuse Hybrid Tea that changes to yellow; 'Livin' Easy', an apricot-orange Floribunda; 'Mt. Hood', an ivory-white Grandiflora; and 'Carefree Delight', a pink-and-white Landscape rose.

Polyanthas bloom continuously and bear large clusters of small flowers.

'Graham Thomas' *is an Austin rose with fully double flowers in the cupped style of Old Garden roses, but with a continuous-blooming habit, strong yellow color, and a sweet fragrance.*

tics of Old Garden roses—very double, cupped or flat, often quartered, and fragrant flowers on compact shrubs with beautiful foliage—that are also continuous bloomers. He calls them English roses, although many people pay him homage by calling them Austin roses. Austin's marvelous creations may look like old Gallicas, Damasks, Bourbons, and Portlands, but their reblooming habit makes them available for landscaping situations where season-long bloom is wanted.

These newer classes of roses, along with Landscape roses such as the Towne and Country, Romance, and Dream series, not only give gardeners more color over the season, but more roses per plant. That means they can be harvested as cut roses for the house without harming the plants or ruining their good looks. Taking a few cuttings, in fact, will only stimulate continuous-blooming roses to produce new shoots.

Very floriferous roses *like the Modern Shrub 'Bonica' make excellent low hedges and walkway borders.* (Helen and Arthur Dawson garden, La Jolla, CA)

Bringing Roses Indoors

When heading out to cut roses for your house, look for a bud that's just beginning to open and is on a shoot that can be cut back without damaging the overall shape of the shrub. In fact, think of cutting roses as a way to spruce up the shape of the bush. Crossed stems, out-of-place stems, and extra-long side stems are all good candidates.

If the rose is a continuous-blooming Hybrid Tea with single blossoms atop long stems, cut far back on the stem (approximately half its length) to where the compound leaves have five leaflets, and make your cut about ¼ inch above an outward-facing bud. This will give you a long stem for the vase (although new research suggests that cutting roses between the swelling behind the bud and the first set of leaves may encourage more repeat bloom). With Floribundas, Polyanthas, and other roses that hold their flowers in sprays or trusses, take the whole spray or truss rather than just remove the stem and opening bud. Several roses in bloom surrounded by tight buds are lovely in a vase.

If the plant makes a single, yearly display in May or June, look for out-of-place shoots with nicely formed flowers and cut the stem back to where the compound leaves begin. This might only be a quarter to a third of the stem's length. Since no more flowers will appear during the year, you'll be stimulating

A simple arrangement of the Grandiflora 'Gold Medal' with a few white peonies and slender blades of a striped Miscanthus turns a minute on the porch into a moment to remember. (Sabrina and Freeland Tanner garden, Yountville, CA)

Take a rose cutting where the compound leaves have five leaflets— just above an outward-facing bud.

the growth of new wood on which roses will bloom the following year.

Choose roses of the same variety to make a formal display in a vase. For a more natural arrangement, choose different kinds of roses with harmonious flower colors, and arrange them with some lacy foliage or frilly flowers, such as fern fronds or baby's breath.

New Climbing Sports of Hybrid Teas

Besides the useful category of the continuous-blooming Modern Climbing roses (which are really just tall shrubs that will act like climbers if given support), many favorite Hybrid Teas have, over the years, developed a genetic mutation that turns them into climbers. They and the Climbing Floribundas need winter protection from Zones 6 north, however, so be forewarned if you live in a region where temperatures drop to zero or below.

The Climbing Hybrid Teas are a very useful advance for gardeners, because these cherished roses can come out of their beds and climb pillars, posts, archways, arbors, and pergolas, or be attached to walls (where they need to be carefully pruned and positioned to prevent their looking too stiff and upright). They will also climb into and display their flowers in medium-sized trees.

Increased Pest and Disease Resistance

Along with better habits and larger sprays of roses, breeders have begun to breed disease and pest resistance into their plants. Much work has been done in environmentally conscious Germany to produce roses that don't have to be sprayed with chemical insecticides or pesticides. Even if you're not particularly organic in your garden practice, these new roses are a welcome development because they cut down on the amount of work required to keep them looking their best.

Healthier rose plants will produce more blossoms than diseased ones, and the foliage will stay attractive. Those who

A Fine Pairing

Varieties of rose of Sharon (*Hibiscus syriacus*) with blue flowers, such as 'Bluebird' and 'Coelestis', make stunning partners for modestly sized, red, continuous-blooming Climbing roses like 'Dublin Bay' or 'Don Juan'.

have tried to grow black-spot-sensitive roses in the East, especially in New England, know exactly what's meant when roses are described as "black spot on a stick." This fungal disease spots the foliage and eventually destroys it, setting back the plant and preventing the development of healthy flowers. Mulching right up to the canes and spraying weekly with a baking-soda solution will help prevent black spot, but if you live in an area where black spot is common, a disease-resistant rose may be your best bet.

One of the first of the new "environmental" roses was the pink 'Flower Carpet', introduced in 1995—a rose generally well accepted for

Healthier rose plants will produce more blossoms than diseased ones, and their foliage will stay attractive.

'Flower Carpet Pink' *anchors a slope planting above a terraced wall. The pink flowers look great against the dark burgundy foliage of a barberry.* (Tomas garden, Napa Valley, CA)

'Dream Pink' *is a trouble-free rose that can be used in out-of-the-way places in the landscape. One of the Dream Series roses, it is also suitable for containers.* (Photo courtesy Anthony Tesselaar International)

its use in the trouble-free landscape, but of a rather hard than dainty pink. It was soon followed by a much prettier soft pink 'Appleblossom Flower Carpet' cultivar, along with 'White Flower Carpet', and in the spring of 2000, 'Red Flower Carpet', which added a welcome, strong red—the most popular of all flower colors—to the series. 'Red Flower Carpet' features softly ruffled, single, 2-inch blooms in sprays that will gently cascade over the edges of a wall or container, or sprawl prettily among other plants in the mixed border. These roses are a deep velvety red with a clutch of golden stamens in their centers. The Flower Carpet series blooms all summer.

The firm of Anthony Tesselaar brought the Flower Carpet series to the United States from Germany, and now has introduced the new Dream series, developed by San Diego rose breeder Jerry Twomey. The first four roses in this series are called 'Dream Pink', 'Dream Yellow', 'Dream Orange', and 'Dream Red'. They were introduced in the spring of 2000. Though not considered disease-proof, they are resistant to black spot and other fungal diseases. They're hardy to Zone 6.

The colors of these four roses are strong, the blooms large (up to 6 inches across), and two are scented: the pink rose has a light, musky fragrance and the yellow a fruity scent. The orange and red varieties aren't scented. Their good points include the disease resistance; a compact, bushy growth habit; a mature height of 3 to 4 feet; bloom from spring to fall; good container performance; and long life when used as a cut flower.

In the landscape, the Dream series' large blooms, bright colors (other colors are in the breeder's pipeline), trouble-free nature, and ease of pruning (cut back to several 10-inch sticks when dormant) make them useful in out-of-the-way landscape spots, but their good container performance means they can be potted up and used beside walls, on patios, and by stairways. One excellent way to use their clear colors to advantage is to make drifts of the different varieties in a large bed with companions like baby's breath (*Gypsophila paniculata*), lambs' ears (*Stachys byzantina*), *Artemisia*, and catmint (*Nepeta* spp.)—interweaving groups of three to five—using the white between the orange and red, and between the red and pink.

These are just two examples of the many new, low-maintenance roses now available. That doesn't mean, however, that plantings should be limited to them. Through the ages, all kinds of roses have been cherished for reasons that still make them loved—and commercially available.

Unrivaled Variety

We love roses because they add beauty to our gardens with a power and elegance like no other plants in the world—first for their cheerful colors, and then for their fragrance. There's nothing coarse or muddy in the sweet, pure smell of a rose. On closer inspection, we discover the beauty of their form—elegant, graceful, refined, and perfectly proportioned.

Single roses can be dramatic in the land-scape, especially when they are carried in huge trusses, as shown by the Modern Shrub 'Marjorie Fair' (left) and Hybrid Musk 'Ballerina' (right).

'Broadway' *is a stunning Hybrid Tea with a unique color blend.*

Roses range from tiny, single blossoms to huge, plate-sized flowers with dozens of petals. Their colors run nearly around the color wheel, though there are no true blue roses (as yet). Some have pretty, nicely shaped and displayed foliage, while others' foliage is best hidden. They grow from just a few inches tall to 25 feet or more.

This unmatched diversity allows for a wide, almost unlimited palette for designing. Is there a spot for a featured rose, growing by itself? How about a rose arbor attached to the side of the house? Can continuous-blooming roses help that perennial bed that tends to go out of flower in July? What do you see from your main windows, and could roses improve the view? Do you want to screen areas from your view, or from your neighbors' view? How about roses growing up the side of a porch or deck? Could roses bring your foundation plantings to life? Is there a wall or fence that would be improved with roses? Are there trees and shrubs that could serve as scaffolding for a climbing rose?

To answer these questions, you'll need a familiarity with the various kinds of roses, how they perform, how to cultivate them, and how to prune them properly for best growth and flowering. Remember, however, that almost all roses have several needs in common—at least six hours of sunlight each day, plenty of water, and good, compost-rich soil.

Form and Foliage

The diversity of rose forms reflects the long history of the genus *Rosa* in the hands of human beings. The wild forms, or species, alone show great differences in height, flower shape, foliage, and so forth—and this is simply the raw material from which rose breeders have created our huge palette of plants.

You can find plenty of short and shrubby roses—the Miniatures, Patios, and procumbent Shrub roses. And tall and shrubby roses—old-

Roses of similar color *are more readable in mixed plantings when separated by a contrasting color. Here, a yellow barberry holds the medium pink Polyantha 'La Marne' (foreground) at arm's length from the Hybrid Musk 'Ballerina' (rear).* (David Dempsey garden, Atlanta, GA)

Shrub roses grow into sturdy bushes that like ample space; most fare nicely in mixed borders.

Rose thorns *can be wickedly painful nuisances, but they also can be ornamental. The pretty prickles of this rose cane are softened by the tiny flowers of baby's breath (Gypsophila paniculata).*

fashioned Noisettes and Albas, big *R. wichurana* hybrids and Grandifloras, among many others. These roses grow into sturdy bushes that like ample space, and most will also fare nicely in a mixed border. By contrast, there are tall and lanky roses like the Eglantines, whose winding stems seem to prefer some form of scaffolding to grow on. Then there are Climbing roses—so called because they can be tied up as though they were climbing, when in reality they have no tendrils or aerial rootlets by which to climb. And then, there are the Rambling roses—huge, vigorous plants that scamper over fences, buildings, and small trees.

Roses range from the wickedly thorny—and the ornamentally thorny, such as 'Red Wing' with its blood-red thorns—to the thornless, such as *R. banksiae* and 'Zéphirine Drouhin'. Their foliage shares in the diversity, also. Some rose foliage, like the *R. rugosa* hybrids, is crinkly and trouble-free, while on others, like the Hybrid Teas, it is glossy and prone to disease. Some foliage is tiny; some is big; and some—like the popular 'Félicité et Perpétue' and the species *R. sempervirens*—is evergreen. Leaves can be bright green, medium green, dark green, blue-green, matted, or shiny.

Perfection of Flower Form

Although roses were prized long ago for their medicinal effects, the ancients appreciated them as beautiful flowers, too. About 3,000 years ago, Homer praised the beauty of the rose (probably *R. canina*, the wild European dog rose) that provided oil to scent the body of the slain Hector. From then until now, mankind still agrees that the rose is, without question, the most popular and beloved flower in the world. Surely its perfection of form is a chief reason.

Roses' pretty buds open slowly to reach a crescendo of beauty at their moment of perfection, and then, all too soon, blow too far open, after which the petals fall and the hips develop. This ineffable "moment of perfection" is in the eye of the beholder, but it occurs in all roses, no matter what their form. Variations of form have developed through the long history of rose cultivation, and involve their fullness, their shape, and their centers.

Rose fullness refers to the number of petals. Most species roses and very old forms are "single," having five to seven petals arranged around the central cluster of stamens. Shakespeare's eglantine (*R. eglanteria*) is a perfect example; its semidouble flowers have eight to 20 petals in two or three rows. There's a form called "loosely double" by some and simply

Rose blossoms *come in many forms. This Modern Shrub rose 'Yellow Jacket' has what's known as an "open-cupped" shape.*
(Chris Wootruba garden, La Mesa, CA)

Pegging Creates Dramatic Effect

Gently bend over long shoots, peg the tips toward, but not touching, the ground, and shorten any side shoots.

Make sure canes do not touch the ground.

Few sights are as striking as a rose that's been "pegged down." This is an English technique not often seen in the United States, but it's easy to do and quite effective in the landscape. A rose that's pegged down has the tips of its long canes tied close to the ground so that they arch out from the central growing point. The canes are evenly spaced around the center so that a large circular mound is created. And because the canes are almost horizontal, receiving strong sunlight along their lengths, the plant will flower along the entire cane. The effect will be that of a large mound absolutely smothered in roses.

Start by planting a Bourbon or Hybrid Perpetual that has been pruned back hard.

Your rose will produce canes reaching 5 to 7 feet. If they stretch out from the roots in a 5-foot radius, the mound will be about 10 feet in diameter, so keep this in mind when selecting a location. The following fall, gently bend the shoots toward the ground, peg the tips with bent-wire hoops or stakes or ties, and shorten. The shoots should be about 2 inches above the ground so they won't take root. Flowers will be sporadic in the first season, but prolific in subsequent years.

'Mary Rose', *a very fragrant rose of warm pink color and a double, old-fashioned shape, is one of the most popular Austin roses.*

"double" by others that has from 21 to 29 petals in three or four rows, and the "fully double" form has 30 to 39 petals in four or more rows. "Very double" refers to roses with 40 or more petals in many rows.

The shape of roses varies widely, too. A "cupped" rose is just that—an open, cuplike form. The "globular" shape is cupped, but with the petal tips curving inward to form a loose globe. The "pompon" is found in very double roses displaying a shaggy puff of short petals. The petals of a "reflexed" rose curve up and out, then down toward the outside, turning the flower almost inside out and forming either a tight or loose ball shape atop the stem. "Rosettes" show petals neatly arranged in a flat circle around the center. Flat flowers whose outer petals are slightly curved upwards are called "saucer" roses.

The centers of roses also have names. A "button" center shows a round eye in the middle of a very double rose. "High-centered" roses have petals that form a conical shape toward the center, such as the familiar Hybrid Teas. Roses with "muddled" centers are at least semi-double, and the petals open this way and that to obscure the stamens. Some single to double roses show an "open" center where the stamens are prominently visible. And finally, some of the most beautiful roses, especially many Old Garden roses and modern Austins, have quartered centers; depending on the variety, the inner petals form three, four, or five very apparent sections when the flowers are fully open. A thin ring of outer petals often charmingly surrounds the quartered centers.

Seasons of Bloom

Gardeners, horticulturists, and rosarians use many terms to indicate a rose's ability to bloom more than once in a season, or the lack of such ability. "Once-blooming" roses are those that produce just one crop of flowers a year, most often in late May to mid-June, depending upon the region and the particular rose. However, there are some once-blooming roses that bloom in late June or even July, and these are referred to as "summer-blooming" roses.

There are numerous terms for roses that bloom more than once. "Repeat-flowering," "recurrent," and "remontant" roses are those that produce a main flush of flowers in spring, and a second, often lighter, flush of flowers in either summer or fall. Those that flower continuously throughout the growing season are called "continuous-blooming" or "perpetual" roses. And, finally, "reblooming" is a general term applied to any rose that blooms more than once—whether it repeats only once or flowers continuously. It should be noted that while these are the most widely accepted definitions for reblooming roses, in common practice, these words are often misused or thrown about without regard to their true meaning—so if in doubt, ask when and how often a rose flowers before purchasing and placing a rose in your landscape.

Because some roses are continuous bloomers, it seems many gardeners want *all* roses to be continuous bloomers. And while that's an understandable desire, it's not realistic and probably never will be (although

The Modern Climbing rose *'America' shows the classic "fully double" shape.*

Quick Guide to Pruning Times

Not all roses are pruned the same. When and how far roses are cut back depends primarily on their flowering habits. Once-blooming roses generally flower on old wood, so prune them in summer after they have finished flowering, and then only lightly to shape or thin. (If you prune them in winter or spring, you'll cut off the flower buds.) Most continuous-blooming roses flower on new wood and should be pruned back by one-third or more in winter or early spring, and then deadheaded throughout the season to encourage new growth and flowering. The exception is Hybrid Teas grown in cold climates. They should be pruned in fall and given ample winter protection. In spring, any dead tips can be trimmed away.

There are some once-blooming roses that bloom in late June or even July; these are referred to as "summer-blooming" roses.

The more strongly a rose reblooms, the more likely it is to be frost tender.

'Europeana'

Choice Roses

for Exceptional Color

'Alchymist' ⑥ This Modern Shrub rose is a hardy Kordes hybrid. It is large, very fragrant, and sports yellow to orange flowers the color of frozen pops. Zone 5.

'Angel Face' ⑥ This Floribunda's lavender-mauve blooms are quite unusual in color. They are scented, fully double, cupped, and held against dark green, leathery foliage. Zone 5.

'Baby Faurax' ⑥ This is a sweet little Polyantha that grows to just over a foot tall and as wide. It features small, dark violet blossoms throughout the growing season. Zone 5.

The cold-hardy 'Alchymist' boasts beautiful yellow to orange blossoms.

"never" is a long time, and with advances in genetic engineering, it's conceivable that the once-blooming old Shrub roses may someday have the genes for continual bloom inserted into their DNA).

We don't fault rhododendrons or viburnums for blooming only once, nor the many other favorite flowering shrubs. And the ability to rebloom comes at a cost. The more strongly a rose reblooms, the more likely it is to be frost tender, demand prompt deadheading, and require protection from pests and diseases. So perhaps we should just be realists and use once-blooming roses without hesitation in our landscape, even though

'Double Delight' ⑥ The creamy petals of this fully double, sweet-scented Hybrid Tea are brushed along the edges with a deep rose-pink. Zone 5.

'Europeana' ⑥ A Floribunda with clusters of double, deep red flowers held against deep hued, greenish-oxblood foliage. Zone 6.

'Graham Thomas' ⑥ This rich yellow English rose is a standout that rightfully honors the 20th century's preeminent plantsman. It blooms continuously, offering fully double, scented flowers. Zone 5.

'Just Joey' ⑥ Imagine a Hybrid Tea with peachy-orange petals fading to a soft pink along their scalloped edges and you'll know 'Just Joey'. Its fully double, fragrant blossoms appear from summer through fall. Zone 5.

'Peace' ⑥ This beloved Hybrid Tea most often has creamy yellow centers with blushing pink edges, but the colors are mutable in different climates and soils, becoming golden edged with red. Zone 5.

'Veilchenblau' ⑥ Called the "Blue Rose" by some, this Multiflora Rambler is actually purplish lavender—perhaps the closest we come to a blue rose. It is fruit-scented and blooms in early summer. Zone 5.

'Westerland' ⑥ A large Floribunda with apricot-orange blossoms. It is a continuous bloomer with bold clusters of scented, double flowers. Zone 5.

'Peace'

they, like many of their companions in the border, will have their season and then retire into quiet green leaf for the remainder of the year.

Fall may bring some surprises, though, for many roses that typically have only one season will put out a small flush of late summer or early fall bloom, especially in the warmer zones; or lacking that, dress themselves in good fall color and hang out brightly colored hips. Here in California, for instance, as well as in much of the southeastern United States, we get two seasons from roses—May and September. In colder regions, June may give the only period of strong bloom.

A Rainbow of Colors

Roses bloom in such a wide range of colors, it's astonishing that most of them coordinate so well with one another. They show almost every flower color except blue (which really isn't very common among other flowers either), and even then, some of the mauve roses make a stab in that direction. Purple—the deep purple of grape juice—is also a stretch.

White roses afford their growers some capabilities that other roses just don't have. For one thing, white goes with everything, and thus can be worked into almost any border or group of roses, especially as a punctuation point to mark the end of one color passage and the beginning of another. In addition, white is a cooling color, and white roses adorning the sunny wall of a house in an area with hot summers is a welcome sight.

Roses also come in multiple forms of color. When the blooms are of one solid color, the color is called "single." When a rose shows "bicolor," it means the petals are different colors on the front and back. A "blend" has two or more colors on the front of each petal, such as the pink-and-cream blend of 'Peaches 'n Cream'. When rose petals show distinct stripes, the color is called, naturally enough, "striped." *Rosa gallica* var. *officinalis* 'Versicolor', with its pale pink and reddish-pink stripes, is a good example.

Some of the most cherished of all roses are blends. 'Peace', perhaps the favorite of all roses, has creamy-yellow to pastel edges. Its color varies depending on the composition of the soil in which it's grown—a characteristic not confined to 'Peace' but which occurs in many roses. One of the advantages of roses with blended petal colors is that you can coordinate both colors with other flowers surrounding it. The pastel yellow of 'Peace' might coordinate with perennials like a cool, pastel yellow yarrow (*Achillea tomentosa*). Its light pink to pinkish-lavender shade would coordinate with the smaller, pink pincushion flower (S. *columbaria* 'Pink Mist'). The fun here is in choosing color combinations yourself—and

Possibly the most ancient of all roses in cultivation, the Apothecary's Rose (**Rosa gallica** var. officinalis) is a once-blooming Old Garden rose so tenacious it remains growing around old foundations in Europe centuries after being planted. *(Berkshire Botanic Garden, Stockbridge, MA)*

One of the advantages of roses with blended petal colors is that you can coordinate both of its colors with other flowers.

The Floribunda 'Angel Face' shows a unique blend of lavender and crimson on its wavy-edged petals.

The flowers of 'Frühlingsgold' carry a clutch of distinctive gold stamens in their centers.

don't be afraid to move the perennials and try something new if the colors don't suit.

Many roses have visible clutches of stamens in their centers—especially single or slightly double types. When these stamens are vivid gold, they're quite noticeable as part of the flower coloration. In some cases, they are dark, running to brownish-reds. For example, the popular Modern Shrub rose 'Lafter' has salmon-pink petals that fade to gold toward its center—a gold that is augmented by the golden stamens visible at its very center. Such noticeable stamens offer a color for coordinating with nearby perennials, too.

Delightful and Diverse Fragrances

What smells as lovely as a rose? Not much. And yet roses don't advertise their fragrance the way orange blossoms or daphnes (*Daphne odora*) do. One must make the effort—put the nose right up to the rose to be re-

warded with that most blissful scent. Although there's not much of the fragrant rose oil in each blossom, it's enough to have entranced humankind for millennia. This attar (or otto as it's sometimes called) is not easily obtained. Six hundred bushels of rose petals are needed to make 1 pound of essential rose oil, and most comes from a few hundred square miles of *R*. x *damascena* plantings in Bulgaria, where the climate is perfect for this species. *R*. x *damascena* gives the fragrance we associate with rose water or rose oil. The oil is extracted from the petals by solvent, and then diluted in alcohol to make perfume (a minimum 19 percent oil), eau de toilette (from 11 to 18 percent), and cologne (between 5 and 10 percent). There is certainly something soothing and innocent, and romantically stimulating, about the classic smell of attar of roses.

Rose scents are not all of a kind, however. Other scents can range from high and sweet, like the note of a flute, to rich and musky, like the sound of an oboe; from rich and sweet, like honey, to thin and sharp, like citrus.

Scent is an evanescent quality. A rose may be heavily scented on a sunny morning, but have comparatively little scent by late in the day. This is because rose petals have specialized glands called osmophores, which produce tiny, scent-filled oil droplets of amazing chemical complexity. A single oil droplet, so small it's almost invisible to the naked eye, can contain up to 400 different organic compounds. Most of these compounds are volatile—that is, they will evaporate in the heat and strong light of a sunny day. That's why the late afternoon rose has lost much of the scent of the morning rose.

During the night, roses will produce more oils, but as the days progress, they finally lose their strong scent. Fresh roses are, therefore, the most fragrant. So, cut your roses for the vase first thing in the morning, when that day's newly opened petals are brimming with fragrance compounds.

Old Garden roses, *like this Gallica 'Cardinal de Richelieu', bred in 1840, tend to have flattened, very double flowers and bloom just once a year.*

Fresh roses are the most fragrant, so cut your roses for the vase first thing in the morning.

Choice Roses
for Exceptional Fragrance

'The Wife of Bath'

R. alba 'Semi-plena' 🌀 This large, shrubby Alba grows to 8 feet with loosely held branches and sweetly fragrant, white, semidouble flowers. Zone 3.

'Comte de Chambord' 🌀 A gorgeous double Portland, with a perfume to match its rich, warm pink color. Makes a dense shrub about 3 feet tall. Zone 5.

'Étoile de Hollande' 🌀 A small, 2-foot Hybrid Tea with deep purplish-pink, semidouble, heavily scented blossoms, often found as its climbing sport. Zone 6.

'Gertrude Jekyll' 🌀 Some say this Austin rose is the most fragrant of all. Its fully double petals crinkle the dark pink, almost red, roses into a globular shape. It blooms from spring to fall. Zone 5.

'Honorine de Brabant' 🌀 This 6-foot-tall Bourbon carries very fragrant, pale lilac flowers with deep purplish markings. Zone 5.

'Kazanlik' 🌀 One of the chief Damasks used in Bulgaria in the manufacture of attar of roses, with that true rose fragrance. Use its loosely double, warm pink petals for your potpourri. Zone 4.

'Königin von Dänemark' 🌀 A 5-foot Alba with small, deep pink, classically quartered flowers that carry a gorgeous perfume. Zone 4.

'Reine des Violettes' 🌀 This is one of the choicest Hybrid Perpetuals, arching 5 feet, with soft, thornless stems and red-violet, perfumed, quartered flowers. Zone 5.

'Rose de Rescht' 🌀 One of the most popular Portlands, this 3-foot shrub emits a heavenly perfume from its red-violet flowers that fade to a pinkish magenta with age. Zone 6.

'The Wife of Bath' 🌀 A truly exquisite English rose with lovely semidouble, blush pink, cupped roses with an unusual clove scent. Grows only to 3 feet. Zone 5.

'Reine des Violettes'

A number of popular roses are exceptionally fragrant. The Austin (or English) rose 'Gertrude Jekyll' is among the most heavily scented. A gardener I know had 50 fragrant roses blooming in her June garden and told me that 'Gertrude Jekyll' won the prize for most fragrance. The Hybrid Tea 'Tiffany' is extremely fragrant, as is 'Hansa', one of the rugosa tribe. 'Mister Lincoln', 'Chrysler Imperial', 'French Perfume', 'Anna Pavlova', 'Fragrant Cloud', and many others carry a gorgeous scent. Among the climbers, 'Souvenir du Docteur Jamain', 'Étoile de Hollande,' and 'Gloire de Dijon' are highly fragrant.

The Most Useful Roses

All roses trace their ancestry back to species that grow wild in various parts of the world. These include species such as *R. wichurana* and *R. rugosa*. The species roses themselves are mostly once blooming and fairly pest and disease resistant, due to their co-evolution with pests and diseases in the wild. Most of the species roses have been hybridized with other species and crosses, so that today we have classes like the *R. wichurana* hybrids and *R. rugosa* hybrids, among others, showing many of their progenitors' traits plus bigger and better bloom.

Gallicas, Damasks, Albas, Centifolias, and Mosses are the oldest types of cultivated roses, known for hundreds, and in some cases, thousands of years. Today, they are known as the Old Garden roses. They are sturdy, hardy, and mostly once blooming, and have made their accommodations with diseases over enough time for them to develop a good resistance. They have been used in the landscape for centuries.

A second group of Old Garden roses was created when European botanists discovered continuous-blooming roses in China and the Far East, and admixed their genes with the European varieties. This resulted in the introduction of Chinas, Portlands, Hybrid Perpetuals, and Tea roses. The Bourbons joined this group after their progenitor was discovered on the Isle de Bourbon in the Indian Ocean. Many of the roses in this second group have the continuous-blooming habit of the Chinas, but are more frost tender. Some are also more prone to disease.

The aptly named 'Joseph's Coat', a Modern Shrub rose (some classify it as a Modern Climbing rose), blooms continuously and will be the star of the landscaping show just about anywhere it's planted.

Old Garden roses grow into large, dense shrubs that need only a light pruning immediately after they bloom to open them up to air and light.

Modern roses, which date from the mid-19th century, include the Hybrid Teas, Floribundas, Grandifloras, Polyanthas, Miniatures, Modern Shrubs, Landscape roses, Modern Climbing roses, and several other classes. These generally combine a little more of the hardiness of the first type of Old Garden roses with the more frequent bloom of the second type and, with the exception of Hybrid Teas, with better disease resistance. Thus, the Modern roses are, in general, more useful in the everblooming, rose-bedecked landscape.

A New Look at Old Garden Roses

Interestingly, while the Old Garden roses were cherished as landscape plants in the 19th century, they were not available in the United States throughout much of the 20th century except as pass-along plants. The newer Modern roses were in such demand that nurseries simply dropped the older roses from their catalogs. Fortunately, revival efforts in the late 1960s once again brought the virtues of these classic roses to the attention of gardeners, and their popularity continues to grow.

Although there is much diversity among Old Garden roses, their fragrance, perhaps more than any other factor, sets them apart from Modern roses. Their colors also tend to be slightly more muted, a characteristic that many (including gardening greats Gertrude Jekyll and Vita Sackville-West) find appealing. And most are quite determined to survive, even when left alone, as evidenced by the

Mix and Mingle

When growing roses on a fence, plant varieties with different colors at intervals so that a horizontal cane of one rose intertwines with a horizontal cane of its neighbor. The mixed color combinations can be striking. Many garden designers caution against pinks with oranges, but if you like the idea, go ahead and do it. You can always move a rose later.

many Old Garden roses that were planted prior to the Civil War but can still be found around old homesteads—many of them abandoned—throughout the Deep South. Old Garden roses usually grow into large, dense shrubs that need only a light pruning immediately after they bloom to open them up to air and light.

Among these old roses handed down to us from more than a hundred years ago, it's important to know their blooming habits, because you will make landscaping choices based on that knowledge. Simply put, the Gal-

The Portlands *are a class of Old Garden roses that bloom more than once a year. 'Comte de Chambord' (foreground) blooms all summer and carries a heady, sweet fragrance.* (Susan Price garden, Petaluma, CA)

A visually appealing picket fence hides the awkward legs of a Hybrid Tea 'Eden', allowing just its flower-filled top to show.
(Susan Price garden, Petaluma, CA)

While no one can argue with the beauty of Hybrid Tea flowers, their leggy, upright, and vigorous habit calls for careful placement in the landscape.

licas, Damasks, Albas, Centifolias, and Moss roses are usually once bloomers, while the Chinas, Portlands, Bourbons, Hybrid Perpetuals, and Tea roses are usually continuous or repeat bloomers. These rebloomers, because most are not as cold tolerant as the once-blooming varieties, are most suitable for warmer climates.

The Mixed Blessing of Hybrid Teas

In 1867, a French breeder named Guillot crossed a Hybrid Perpetual (thought to be 'Mme. Victor Verdier') with a Tea rose (some say 'Mme. Falcot', others say 'Mme. Bravy') and produced the Hybrid Tea 'La France'. It is from the introduction of 'La France' that we date the era of Modern roses. It soon became apparent that with 'La France' and other Hybrid Teas that soon followed, a new and different kind of rose had entered the picture. Hybrid Teas gained in popularity over the last half of the 19th century and dominated rose growing through most of the 20th century.

Hybrid Teas are now strong, upright bushes with long stems ending in single flowers, as opposed to the more graceful old shrubs that hold their flowers in clusters. The buds of Hybrid Teas are high-centered and scroll open into a convex rather than flat-faced form. Their petals are sturdy and often shiny. Over the ensuing 130-plus years, breeders have introduced thousands of new Hybrid Tea roses. The vigor of the plant, the haughty beauty of its flower form, and the strength of its colors account for the popularity of Modern Hybrid Teas.

While no one can argue with the beauty of the individual flowers—one look at 'Ophelia' and your heart will melt—their leggy, upright, and vigorous habit calls for careful placement in the landscape. Their colors—which can be pure and soft, but which can also be hard and garish—also need to be chosen and used judiciously. They are hardy only to Zone 7, and even then need some protection. Unlike many other

Modern roses, they are susceptible to pests and diseases, and thus require good air circulation and routine care.

Polyanthas Make Petite Edgers

Polyanthas are continuous-blooming roses with fine, usually shiny leaves and bear large clusters of small, 1-inch flowers that range from single to double in form. Because they only grow to about 2 feet tall and display pretty foliage, they make fine foreground plants in a border and excellent low hedges. They are also among the best roses for trouble spots like the bottom of a bare garage wall. Polyanthas are relatively disease resistant and hardy to Zone 6. And best of all for the landscape, they are low-maintenance roses that need only the removal of dead or very old shoots to keep them in shape.

Polyanthas, because they only grow to about 2 feet tall and display pretty foliage, make fine foreground plants in a border and excellent low hedges.

Several specimens *of the pink Polyantha 'The Fairy' make a low hedge along the edge of a bed bordering the lawn.*

Classes of Roses

The Noisette 'Champneys' Pink Cluster' spills through an oakleaf hydrangea (Hydrangea quercifolia).
(Pat and Stan Henry garden, Laurens, SC)

Here's a quick look at the various classes of roses, any of which you might find in a nursery or catalog. The Floribundas, Modern Shrubs, and Landscapes are the most useful roses for hedging, foundation plantings, and mixed beds and borders. The Climbers and Ramblers are used to cover arbors, trellises, and fences, as well as to grow up posts, around windows, and into trees. Miniature and Patio roses are especially suited to pots, window boxes, hanging baskets, and other tight spaces.

Albas—Tough but beautiful ancient roses, most with excellent fragrance. They flower in lovely pastel shades and, because of their high disease resistance, mix well with other plants. They're once blooming and when their display is finished, they step back to take a quiet place in the border.

Bourbons—Discovered on what is now the island of Reunion in the Indian Ocean in 1817, they soon became a favorite rose of our 19th-century forebears. Most are once blooming, but many repeat in autumn. Bourbons are very fragrant, and their flowers generally have the classic "old rose" appearance.

Centifolias—Once-blooming, winter hardy, and very double European roses (called the cabbage rose) with delightful fragrance. One of the most exquisitely formed and proportioned of the Old Garden roses.

Chinas—Their continuous-blooming habit has been transferred into almost all our Modern, continuous-blooming roses. They make up for their stalky, sparsely leaved growth with an abundance of sweetly scented flowers. They are disease resistant, but hardy only to Zone 7.

Climbers—These tall, arching roses with stiff stems don't really climb at all. But they do stretch to 10, 20, and even 25 feet and can be trained against a wall, fence, or trellis. Some belong to a class of Modern Climbing roses, while others are simply sports of nonclimbing roses with especially long canes.

Damasks—Shrubby roses known 3,000 years ago, with a true rose scent. They're usually once blooming, with exquisitely formed flowers. They form medium-sized shrubs that need very little pruning.

Eglantines—Large, prickly-stemmed shrubs with mostly single roses. They are descended from a wild European species and are very hardy.

Floribundas—Large, free-branching shrubs with mostly single roses. They're once blooming, very hardy, need little pruning, and have a lovely apple scent to their foliage.

Gallicas—Small, fragrant, "old rose" flowers bloom once a year on hardy, clumping shrubs. Known since classical antiquity, their genes are in most of our Modern roses. Most are medium-sized, but a few will grow to 10 feet or more.

Grandifloras—These semihardy (Zone 7) roses combine the large-flowered beauty of Hybrid Teas with the stature and copious flowering habit of Floribundas. In fact, in Britain, they are classed as Floribundas.

Hybrid Perpetuals—Fairly hardy roses bred in the mid-1800s, with a continuous-blooming habit that reveals their China heritage. Many are very fragrant, and they range in size from about 4 to 8 feet tall. These were the prize roses of Victorian exhibition halls.

Hybrid Teas—Gorgeous, often fragrant roses appear singly all summer at the ends of shoots on upright, ungainly plants. They are hardy only to Zone 7, and then with some winter protection. They make up for their faults with classic, stunningly beautiful, high-centered blooms.

Landscape roses—A new, catchall category that contains many extremely useful, multihybrids with superior characteristics. These low-maintenance shrubs are continuous blooming, make fine edging and hedging, and don't require fussy pruning.

Miniatures—As the name suggests, these shrub roses grow only 12 to 30 inches tall. Because of their continuous-blooming habit, they should be pruned back each winter. They are hardy only to Zone 7.

Modern Shrub roses—This is another catchall category that covers everything from Ground Cover roses to Hybrid Musks. All are very easy to grow. Includes hybrids of *R. moyesii, R. rugosa,* and *R. spinosissima,* as well as Austins, Bucks, Explorers, Kordesiis, Meidilands, Meillands, Parklands, and Poulsens. The Bucks, Explorers, Kordesiis, and Poulsens are generally very hardy and suited to the northern tier of states, and even parts of Canada. Most are continuous blooming or remontant, disease resistant, and fragrant.

Mosses—Bred from Centifolias and Damasks, these hardy plants have fine, brownish, hairy growth on the flower buds and stem ends. They tend to be once blooming, very fragrant, and shrubby, growing 3 to 5 feet tall.

Noisettes—Bourbon, China, Musk, and Tea roses are in the heritage of Noisettes, which are graceful climbers with a continuous display of fragrant clusters of small roses. Many are tall enough to use on pillars and against trellising, and will bloom quite well even in partial shade.

Patios—These roses are somewhere between Miniatures and compact Floribundas in height. They are quite floriferous with small, continuously produced flowers, often with a mild fragrance. They're excellent grown in containers.

'New Dawn', a climbing R. wichurana hybrid, beautifies an arbor.

Polyanthas—Bred from Multiflora roses over a hundred years ago, these hardy roses have small, attractive leaves and continuously produce large clusters of blooms on bushy plants. They're especially useful in mixed borders, where they drape their flower clusters among the perennials.

Portlands—Repeat blooming and hardy to Zone 6, Portlands (especially the red varieties) were very popular in the mid-1800s. They are usually compact, fragrant, and continuous blooming. They have the classic look of Old Garden roses.

The white Floribunda 'Saratoga' and pink Hybrid Tea 'Fragrant Cloud' kick off a parade of color along this rose border.
(Duke Gardens, Durham, NC)

Ramblers—Most of these large, long-caned roses bloom once on 10- to 15-foot canes, although a few are continuous bloomers. As a class, they adapt to light shade better than other roses.

Species—These are the wild progenitors of all roses, and quite a few are worthy of space in the garden. Some of the most useful are *R. laevigata, R. banksiae, R. hugonis, R. glauca, and R. setigera.* Those from eastern Asia, Europe, and North America tend to be once bloomers, although a few are continuous bloomers. Some can grow to enormous sizes.

Teas—These high-centered roses carry a tea like scent. Many are either continuous bloomers or repeat bloomers. They are one of the progenitors of Hybrid Teas, although their flowers aren't usually as large or classically shaped. Most are 3 to 4 feet tall, but some reach 8 feet or more.

The Diversity of Roses

The brightness *of the Floribunda 'Apricot Nectar' and the fuchsia-colored perennial* **Watsonia** *form a strong focal point in a woods' edge border.* (Sutter Home Vineyard garden, St. Helena, CA)

Among the most popular Polyanthas are 'Cécile Brünner', which has both shrubby and climbing varieties; 'Perle d'Or', with beautiful creamy yellow to light apricot blooms; and 'The Fairy', with scads of double, pink flowers and masses of pretty, shiny, finely textured leaves.

Floribundas Excel in the Landscape

Of the Modern roses, Floribundas are the best group for most landscaping situations, as they are hardy, free flowering, bushy in form, and have the ability to keep an area in color throughout the growing season. They make gorgeous specimen plants, are fine companions with other shrubs and herbaceous flowers in a bed or border, and cover an area with bloom when massed.

The free-flowering Floribundas grow 24 to 48 inches tall, and their dense habit makes them excellent for low hedging. Different varieties produce sprays of single, semidouble, or double flowers in all standard rose colors—sometimes with fragrance—throughout the growing season.

The bushy plants are attractive, which makes them a good choice for massed plantings. Because their blossoms are so pretty and frequent, they're also a good choice as a specimen plant among a bed of other kinds of plants.

Some of the most popular garden roses of all time are Floribundas. 'Gruss an Aachen', my favorite shell-pink rose, the pure white 'Iceberg', and the lovely pink 'Queen Elizabeth' are Floribundas. All are exceptionally hardy, tolerate many landscape conditions, show good disease resistance, flower freely and generously over a long period, and have a beautiful flower form. And while Floribundas vary, it is these characteristics that mark the class and make them so useful in the landscape.

Roses are strongest visually against a contrasting backdrop. Here, the brilliant cerise Grandiflora 'Fame!' serves as backdrop to a slightly smaller Floribunda 'French Lace'. (Joann Romano garden, San Diego, CA)

'Marmalade Skies' is one of three All-America Rose Selections winners for 2001. It's a Floribunda with brilliant tangerine-orange blooms that open from the beginning to the end of the growing season. Olive-green, satiny foliage makes a perfect backdrop for this new rose. It produces five to eight flowers in clusters on each stem, and each flower is about 3 inches across with up to 25 petals. At 3 feet by 3 feet, it's an excellent choice for a hedge, rose bed, or mixed border—anywhere strong color is needed. This rose is highly rated for disease resistance, hardiness, and color, and has many other desirable traits.

Another Floribunda worth mentioning is 'Showbiz'. It's a 1985 All-America Rose Selections winner with bright scarlet flowers that keep coming through the entire season if spent blooms are trimmed off. It can turn a dull corner of the garden or foundation planting into a flashing success. Give it even more power by massing three plants together and pairing them with the pale, pastel yellow of long-blooming, thread-leaved tickseed (*Coreopsis verticillata* 'Moonbeam') and the clear blue of *Geranium* 'Johnson's Blue'.

Make a Rose Cage

When using Floribundas in a mixed border that may get crowded, lift the rose canes vertically—using a rose cage—until they rise above the surrounding plantings. Similar to a tomato cage, a rose cage is a wire frame through which the rose grows and to which it can be tied. When the rose spills over the top, the cage should be obscured, especially if there are other flowers planted at its feet.

Floribundas worth noting for their all-around usefulness in masses, as hedges, and as specimen plantings include the single-flowered, pink to pinkish-mauve varieties 'Betty Prior', 'Escapade', and 'Nearly Wild'; the mauve 'Lilac Charm'; the red 'Europeana'; the golden 'Sunsprite'; the apricot 'Apricot Nectar'; and the white 'Iceberg'.

Grandifloras Flaunt Big, Colorful Flowers

When Hybrid Teas were crossed with Floribundas, the Grandifloras appeared. They grow from 4 to 6 feet tall, and so are useful backing up shorter roses or other plants, or mixing with once-blooming woody shrubs like *Weigela* or *Spiraea*. They produce large, Hybrid Tea-like, crowned flowers in all the rose colors, and bloom all summer. You'll find them reliably hardy to Zone 7, and into Zone 6 with winter protection, much like Hybrid Teas.

Roses in the orange part of the color spectrum seem to be in vogue these days. One of three All-America Rose Selections winners for 2001 is a Grandiflora, 'Glowing Peace,' named after 'Peace,' one of its grandparents. Its plump, 3-inch roses have up to 42 petals that blend yellow and cantaloupe colors. The glossy foliage turns a rich burgundy in the

Miniatures are perfect for containers, as 'Blue Mist' proves. The rose-filled planting box turns a rather awkward passage alongside the house into an inviting little garden.
(Joy Wolff garden, Healdsburg, CA)

fall. It grows 4 feet tall by 3 feet wide and is disease resistant. 'Love', 'Pink Parfait', and 'Queen Elizabeth' are three other popular Grandifloras.

Miniatures for Edgings and Containers

Miniatures are most likely descended from a compact sport of *R. chinensis*. A few enjoyed popularity in the early 19th century but fell out of favor and were lost in Victorian times. They were rediscovered in 1918 and hybridizing began to give us our modern Miniatures, which have really become established only since the end of World War II. Miniatures today are considered Modern roses because in the very hybridized form in which we know them, they have been in commerce only recently.

Miniature roses suit their name, usually growing only 1 or 2 feet tall, with small flowers, usually under 2 inches across. They're useful in planters and in the front of beds and borders. Since they're down at foot level, they're a good choice for edging sunny stretches of steps, and for accenting beds of other roses. They're hardy—to Zone 5— and need pruning only to maintain a proper shape. Most are rebloomers.

Some of the all-time favorite Miniatures include 'Jeanne Lajoie', a medium pink climbing mini (yes, there are climbing types for delicate enhancement of small fences or posts); blends such as 'Magic Carrousel', in red and white, and 'Party Girl', in apricot and yellow; orange-red 'Starina'; white 'Popcorn' and 'Simplex'; and yellow 'Sunshine Girl'.

Only five Miniature roses have ever been given the All-America Rose Selections top award, including a new one introduced for 2001, 'Sun Sprinkles'. It has strong disease resistance, bright yellow blooms

During those periods *when few perennials are blooming in the mixed border, an exquisite rose like the Hybrid Musk 'Penelope' can maintain high interest.*

Since they're down at foot level, Miniature roses are a good choice for edging sunny stretches of steps.

The big, plump flowers of the Floribunda 'Climbing Gold Badge' decorate the upright post of an arbor with naturally silvered wood.

The vigor, size, continuous-blooming habit, and lovely colors of Modern Climbing roses make them marvelously practical in the landscape—on pillars, over arbors, on trellising, up walls, and splayed out along fences.

all season, and, if you can get your nose to them, a spicy fragrance with musky overtones.

Hybrid Musks for Rich Fragrance

These wonderfully useful roses appeared in the first quarter of the 20th century and became an instant hit with rose growers everywhere. They grow 4 to 6 feet tall and bloom continuously with soft-colored, musk-scented blossoms. In the landscape, they are good in borders; make excellent specimens, shrubs, and hedges; do well in containers; and are hardy to Zone 6. Because they're continuous bloomers, thin out older canes in the dormant season and trim back the canes by a third. And because they keep on blooming, they need a rich soil with good nutrition to assist them.

Of all the Hybrid Musks, I like 'Buff Beauty' the best. The color of this double rose is a soft buff-yellow with hints of apricot, and it's nicely scented. It grows about 4 feet tall, making a vigorous shrub. 'Ballerina' is another choice Hybrid Musk, making a 4-foot plant with single, pink roses with white centers.

Modern Climbing Roses

The old-fashioned climbing roses were seldom continuous blooming, although some of the continuous-blooming Old Garden roses developed climbing sports with extra-long canes. But in recent decades, a new development has brought us Modern Climbing roses. These aren't climbing in the sense that they have tendrils or aerial rootlets, or twine around structures. But they are tall, continuous-blooming sports

of Hybrid Teas or other classes—probably descended primarily from *R. multiflora* with a mixture of genes from many other types. One plants them by a framework or structure and ties them up as they grow, usually from 10 to 15 feet tall. Their vigor, size, continuous-blooming habit, and lovely range of colors make them marvelously practical in the landscape—on pillars, over arbors, on trellising, up walls, and splayed out along fences.

Choice varieties of Modern Climbing roses include the salmon-red 'America'; 'Constance Spry', with her clear pink blossoms; the golden-yellow 'Golden Showers'; the deep red 'Don Juan'; and the dark red 'Sympathie'.

Growing two different roses together over a structure is an excellent idea if they are as carefully selected as the deep violet-purple Gallica 'Cardinal de Richelieu' and the Modern Climbing rose 'Alchymist'. (Michael Bates garden, Santa Rosa, CA)

Two continuously blooming Austin roses— the pale 'Yellow Button' and the Gallica-like 'Prospero'—will anchor this border all season. *(Sabrina and Freeland Tanner garden, Yountville, CA)*

Modern Shrub Roses

Modern Shrub roses are very much like Modern Climbing roses in that they carry a mixture of genes from many different varieties, but they grow only from 3 to 8 feet, with most around 5 feet tall. They are vigorous, continuous blooming, and carry as many worthwhile traits as the hybridizers can work into them, especially a tendency to produce clusters of flowers. As a catchall class, they are among the most useful roses for the landscape. Because they are continuous bloomers, they need to be pruned in the dormant season. Like the Hybrid Musks, they make excellent hedges, can be trained to a pillar or post, perform beautifully on a fence, stand alone as specimens, and perform well as anchors in the mixed border.

Some of the most justifiably famous of these Modern Shrubs are the frilly, pink-blossomed 'Bonica'; the blood-red 'Copenhagen'; the red, pink and yellow multicolored 'Joseph's Coat'; the pastel coral-pink Buck hybrid 'Prairie Princess'; and the single, white to blush-pink 'Sally Holmes'. There's also a subset of Modern Shrubs called Procumbent Shrub roses that make excellent ground covers and grow from 12 to 30 inches tall.

Much has been said and written about David Austin's remarkable achievement in hybridizing a group of Modern Shrub roses, but they are certainly worth mentioning again. These English roses, as they are called, have the lovely forms and habits of the Old Garden roses— flat-faced, quartered, and very double blossoms typical of older roses like Gallicas, Mosses, and Damasks—but continuously produce flowers of exquisite scent and luscious colors. Fragrant, pink 'Gertrude Jekyll'; soft pink 'Heritage'; yellow 'Graham Thomas'; pinkish-apricot 'Abraham Darby'; crimson 'L.D. Braithwaite'; and shell-pink, myrrh-scented 'Wife of Bath' are a few of the best. With their attractive form and improved pest and disease resistance, they are especially suitable for mixed beds and borders, or anywhere in the border that shrubs with a nice habit and season-long color would be useful.

Low-Maintenance Landscape Roses

Landscape roses is a catchall category that includes new lines of very trouble-free shrubs, similar to Modern Shrubs. In fact, some question

The Modern Shrub rose 'Carefree Delight' is massed to create a cheerfully floriferous ground cover that needs very little maintenance over the whole growing season.

where Modern Shrub and Landscape roses differ. If anything, Landscape roses require even less maintenance. They rarely need to be sprayed or pruned, and will bloom reliably year after year. They are suitable for hedges, mixed borders, foundation plantings, property boundaries, and even the vegetable garden. They can serve as focal points, as backdrops for other plantings or, in the case of smaller varieties, as edging for beds and borders. Since most are continuous bloomers, you can count on them delivering color throughout the season.

The house of Meidiland in France has been particularly successful in breeding lines of landscape roses. Three of their best are 'Sevillana', with its bright red, double roses on dense, 3-foot shrubs (great for a massed planting); the new sport 'Pearl Sevillana', with creamy white, double flowers blushed with light pink; and the old standby, 'Cherry Meidiland', with single flowers of cerise red with white centers on a 6-foot shrub that never needs pruning. Other garden workhorses in the Landscape category include the Romantica, Renaissance, Tuscan, and Generosa series of roses.

Chapter 3

Around the House

The bright red Floribunda 'Impatient' (right) softens the brick steps at the entry to this house. The rose's color coordinates with other flowering plants, including the foamy, white sweet alyssum (Lobularia maritima) spilling over the brick wall at the bottom. (Ruth Meehl garden, San Diego, CA)

R OSES ARE THE FAVORITE plants of gardeners around the world for good reason. No other plants suggest the bountiful beauty and pleasure of nature the way roses do. Red roses growing on a white picket fence surrounding a rose-covered cottage are the visual metaphor for a happy home. That's because roses are symbols of love and contentment. How wonderful, then, when we actually use roses around our house to bring that metaphor to life!

We can work roses into the foundation plantings that anchor a house to the ground, grow them

85

A staggered planting *of pink roses beautifully ties the house to the landscape. The Floribunda 'Johann Strauss' is the foreground shrub, backed by the sprawling Austin 'Constance Spry' trained to the house wall. A rich blue Delphinium adds the right accent to set off the pinks.* (Joanne Woodle garden, Peconic, NY)

up walls and around windows, edge a driveway with them, and use them to direct foot traffic down a path. They can brighten window boxes, fill pots on the patio or deck with color, and twine happily up porch posts. It's almost impossible to have too many roses around the house if they're chosen to reflect a refined taste.

Roses Brighten Foundation Plantings

Foundation plantings were originally designed to hide a home's foundation—that unattractive base of poured cement or concrete block that supports most houses—but they also serve several other roles in the landscape. Perhaps most importantly, they visually anchor the house to the surrounding landscape. Without them, a house is simply perched on a patch of earth. Foundation plantings provide a living transition from the vertical walls of a house to the lawn and outlying plantings. If the walls or verandas are covered with vines and climbing roses, or surrounded by small trees, the house can almost seem to grow naturally from the landscaping.

Foundation plantings offer a good way to soften the hard edges of the house—both the vertical edges where walls meet and the horizontal edges where porches attach, large windows are set into walls, or roof meets wall. Thus, corners are places where trees or shrubs have the most effect. I prefer evergreens at the corners, so their softening effect continues even through the dormant months.

A hot, humid day will seem cool and refreshing where the white Floribunda 'Iceberg' is paired with the fragrant, white-flowered mock orange (**Philadelphus spp.**) along the foundation of a wall. *(Orene Horton garden, Columbia, SC)*

Add Some Flowering Plants

Most often, foundation plantings are a dull mix of evergreen shrubs like yews (*Taxus* spp.) and junipers (*Juniperus* spp.). By adding some flowering shrubs and perennials, foundation plantings become much more interesting. And by adding roses, they are brought to vigorous life. That's because those evergreens form an excellent backdrop for the bright, colorful flowers of roses. Choose continuous-blooming roses, and you'll have a

Foundation plantings visually anchor a house to the surrounding landscape and soften the hard edges of a house.

Splashes of color look good coming up the drive and when seen through a window of the house, so when designing your foundation plantings, don't forget to consider the vistas from within.

Play with Depth Perception

If there's a brightly colored rose in the foundation planting right outside a window, repeat that color in the distance—for instance, in a border across the lawn. The repetition gives visual coherence to the scene. If there's a very long vista—say 50 yards or more—choose a variety slightly more saturated in color than the one close at hand. Long distances soften the effects of color, so you'll need a rose with a little more punch.

Of course, if the vista is short and you want to create the illusion of greater depth, simply plant a lighter-hued rose in the far border. For instance, if you're using the bright pink Floribunda 'Queen Elizabeth' as the foundation planting, and there's a rather short expanse of lawn to a border, you can give the impression of greater depth by choosing a lighter pink rose like the old Shrub rose 'Fantin-Latour' or the Hybrid Tea 'First Prize' for the border.

The shrubby Hybrid Perpetual *'La Reine' nicely hides the foundation of this house. Its rich but cool pink harmonizes with the violet-blue of catmint* (**Nepeta** *'Six Hills Giant'*). *(Susan Price garden, Petaluma, CA)*

blaze of color in your foundation planting all summer long, even as the flowering shrubs and perennials around them fade into and out of bloom.

As a rule of thumb, I prefer about two thirds of the foundation plants to be an interesting mix of trees and evergreen shrubs that look as good in winter as they do in summer, and the remaining third to be a combination of roses, other deciduous shrubs, and perennials for a superb color show in summer. Not only do these splashes of color look good coming up the drive, but when seen through a window from inside the house, they can brighten the view of your yard. So when designing your foundation plantings, don't forget to consider the vistas from within.

Your choice of rose color for foundation plantings should be consistent with the subtleties of the evergreens and other deciduous shrubs you've chosen, and with the color of your home. A yellow Shrub rose like 'Graham Thomas' can intensify a yellowish-green juniper. Similarly, a luscious, pink rose can bring a brick wall to life. When it comes to bright colors, less can be more. Use very bright roses as accents or to call attention to a focal point such as the front door, a bay window, or some other interesting architectural element. White roses harmonize with any color, so use them freely. And they are especially pleasing against a backdrop of dark evergreen shrubs, where they will brighten the scene.

Foundation plantings *don't have to be just rows of shrubs. Here the large-flowered Climber 'Albertine' graces a window and dresses a stone wall while other shrubs, grasses, and perennials create a contrast of leaf form and size.* (Mr. and Mrs. George Edwards garden, Rock House, Gloucestershire, England)

Two 'Iceberg' Floribundas *trained as standards frame the entrance steps for a stone patio. The arbor is draped in a white-flowered potato vine (Solanum jasminoides), while sweet alyssum (Lobularia maritima) scatters its starry flowers at the feet of the roses.* (Carol Brewer garden, El Cajon, CA)

When mixing roses with other flowering shrubs or perennials, make the rose the dominant visual element. Rose colors are usually standouts anyway, so play to their strengths and site them in visually important places— such as next to the front steps or beneath a picture window. It's also a good idea to repeat the same rose in several places along the foundation because it gives coherence to the design and draws the eye along the planting to other parts of the yard or garden. If you do repeat the same rose, vary the distances between them so that the rhythm of their intervals is syncopated, rather than repetitious.

Dress Up Your Front Door

One place where you might want to consider featuring a particularly favorite rose is over a front or side door. Plant a rose that will grow to about 12 feet. It should be one of the less vigorous roses, or one that you can easily keep to just a few canes. Train the canes up the wall beside the door along some wire and bring them over the top; trim away any sprawling canes that can interfere with access to the door. A continuous-blooming, fragrant rose is best, so you can inhale its perfume as you walk by. My personal choice would be 'New Dawn' or 'Pink Perpetue', but there are many others to choose from.

Roses make a fine transition from a group of foundation plants to an arbor attached to the house. Start with one or two low-growing roses backed by a taller Floribunda or Modern Shrub rose, and then allow a climber to scale the heights of the arbor. This building up of layers gives the Climbing rose a garden out of which to grow, and emphasizes the foundation plantings. It's a very different look from an arbor with the uprights left bare except for the thick stems of the climber, which makes the arbor look a little top-heavy.

Choice Roses

for Foundation Plantings

Poulsen Roser ApS is a major Danish rose firm that has introduced a line of low-care, highly floriferous roses called the Towne & Country series that are perfect for foundation plantings. They drop their spent, double blossoms, are highly disease-resistant (in fact, purchasers are asked *not* to spray them), winter hardy, and can be sheared by a third each February. The first seven roses in this list are Poulsens.

'Coral Gables' ✆ The salmon-coral, double flowers are 2 to 3 inches across and carry a light, wild-rose scent. The plant grows into a compact shrub about 4 feet tall. Zone 5.

'Kent' ✆ Abundant, semidouble, white flowers are profusely borne on 3-foot plants. Zone 5.

'Lexington' ✆ A freely branching rose to 2 feet or so is a great ground cover and produces warm yellow blossoms with a wild-rose scent. Zone 5.

'Madison' ✆ This compact, little bush grows 2 feet tall and wide, making it perfect for the front of a mixed border. It has small, pink, semidouble blossoms. Zone 5.

'Monticello' ✆ This is a rose for southern climates, as the semidouble, warm pink flowers hold well in the heat. It grows to about 3 feet. Zone 5.

'Nashville' ✆ This rose bears large clusters of semidouble, rosy-red flowers with streaks of pink along the petals. It grows 2 to 3 feet tall. Zone 5.

'Tumbling Waters' ✆ A compact, 2-foot shrub for the front of the border. It has gorgeous, delicately ruffled, single, white-with-pink-blush flowers that look like butterflies flitting around the bush. Zone 5.

'Gruss an Aachen' ✆ For nearly a century, this shell-pink beauty of a fragrant Floribunda has been a perfect choice for mixing with perennials and other shrubs in a foundation planting. It tolerates some shade and blooms profusely all summer. Zone 4.

'Tamora' ✆ This Austin rose has the hardiness, disease-resistance, and adaptability that's needed in a great mixed foundation planting. It produces scads of cupped, apricot blooms all summer and grows to about 3 feet tall. Zone 4.

'Yves Piaget' ✆ One of Meilland's new Romantica series of star performers. This one has large, double, very fragrant, rich pink flowers with frilly edges so that they resemble peonies. It blooms continuously on a 2- to 3-foot shrub for the front of the foundation planting. Zone 6.

'Tamora'

French doors are rendered even more French by the Polyantha sweetheart rose ('Climbing Cécile Brünner') that covers their top. *(Maggie Svenson garden, Charlotte, NC)*

An arbor attached to the house elevates 'Rêve d'Or', a Noisette rose of buff to pale yellow, and adds immeasurably to the charm of this house. *(Michael Bates garden, Santa Rosa, CA)*

Flank a Path with Color

Lining a pathway to your front door or a driveway to your house with roses is a great way to welcome guests, whether it's for the first or hundredth time. A row of roses with hues of slight variation creates a simple, classic look that is very appealing. By contrast, an assortment of brightly colored roses can sound a cheerful and exciting note. Plant them along a driveway to give arriving guests a rousing welcome. The farther the viewing distance, the more extravagant the color combinations can be. The approach to Erin and Matt Cline's winery in Sonoma, California, is a half-mile of continuous-blooming Modern Shrub roses in every color of the rainbow. It's a cheerful sight as you approach the winery's tasting room. But even the walkway to an individual's front door can be jazzed up with brightly colored roses.

Hybrid Teas of strong scent are a good choice to mix into the edging for a well-used walkway, as these roses will bloom continuously all summer and will beg to have their fragrance sampled by those who walk the path. Use them here and there rather than as hedging, for which they aren't particularly suited. Hide their bare ankles with soft, blue-flowered mounds of catmint (*Nepeta* × *faassenii*); the intricately patterned leaves of *Artemisia* 'Silver Brocade'; or the silver-gray foliage 'Silver Carpet' lambs' ears (*Stachys byzantina* 'Silver Carpet'), which is a cultivar that doesn't produce flower stalks. Hybrid Teas can also be grown behind low hedges of dwarf boxwood (such as *Buxus sempervirens* 'Suffruticosa') or germander (*Teucrium chamaedrys*) to hide their legginess. Be careful not to shade or crowd Hybrid Teas when sandwiching them between other plants, as this will increase their susceptibility to disease and decrease flowering.

*A **birdbath** anchors the corner of this pleasant, rose-bedecked path. The roses are (left to right) the large, pink-flowered Hybrid Tea 'Tiffany', the yellow-blend Modern Shrub Rose 'Flutterbye', the apricot Floribunda 'Brass Band', and the crimson Floribunda 'Sarabande'.* (French Laundry Restaurant, Yountville, CA)

Plant roses along a driveway to give arriving guests a rousing welcome.

Polyanthas *are a fine rose for a mixed perennial border along a front path. Here* **'The Fairy'** *very effectively throws its trusses of small, pink flowers among its blue companions.* (Jane Miller garden, Palo Alto, CA)

If Hybrid Teas, despite their loveliness, demand more attention than you can give or if you live in colder zones (Hybrid Teas require winter protection in Zones 6 and colder), consider Floribundas and Modern Shrub roses. The Floribundas bear single to fully double, sometimes scented flowers throughout the growing season on upright, often prickly canes. Modern Shrub roses are a diverse group, but usually a bit larger

than the Hybrid Teas. Many bloom continuously, and the flowers are often scented. Both the Floribundas and Modern Shrub roses are hardier and more disease-resistant than Hybrid Teas.

Plant a Hedge

It's fine to vary the flower color in rows of roses, but they will look best if the roses are all about the same height and shape. One option is to edge your driveway or pathway with a hedge of roses.

Old Garden roses—such as Albas, Centifolias, and Gallicas, which generally bloom only once—lend themselves to this treatment. Plant them about 30 inches apart so that their canes will intertwine. Old Garden roses bloom on old wood and don't take well to shearing, so simply remove any canes over three years old and lightly pinch the remaining canes to shape the hedge.

Many continuous bloomers—most notably the Floribundas, Hybrid Musks, Modern Shrub roses, Polyanthas, and *R. rugosa* hybrids—are also suitable for growing as hedges. Because they must be cut back each winter, the hedge will regrow each spring. However, they can be easily sheared throughout the season to maintain their shape. As a general rule, Hybrid Teas don't perform well as hedges, most notably because their strict upright habit renders them ugly in a hedge.

Old Garden roses bloom on old wood and don't take well to shearing, so simply remove any canes over three years old and lightly pinch the remaining canes to shape a hedge.

Dark Leaves Show Off Pink Roses

The dark, purplish leaves of smoke bush (*Cotinus coggygria* 'Royal Purple'), many of the barberries (especially *Berberis thunbergii* 'Rose Glow'), and the purpleleaf sand cherry (*Prunus × cistena*) are prime backdrops for pink roses, especially floriferous Polyanthas like 'The Fairy' and 'Nathalie Nypels'.

If you want a very low rose hedge, choose Patio or Miniature roses. Because these low roses are less noticeable, use varieties with brightly colored flowers or vary their hues. I especially love the bright yellow blossoms of 'Bit O' Sunshine', the red-orange flowers of 'Fashion Flame', and the red-and-white-striped petals of 'Stars 'n' Stripes'—all Miniatures. Colorful Patio roses include the bright red 'Hotline', coral-orange 'Coral Reef', bright orange-red 'Orange Sunblaze', bright yellow 'Golden Sunblaze', and red 'Napa Valley'.

Along Winding Paths

An alternative to edging a path with rows of roses is to allow your path to wind through beds of roses or mixed plantings, a strategy much more suitable for an informal landscape. Small trees can be tucked into the curves of such paths, and roses can be trained up into them. If the path is straight, plant drifts of roses and perennials that cross it at oblique angles. And consider placing a rose-covered pillar somewhere along the path; perhaps it is a lamppost that throws a warm glow into the garden at night.

Continuous flowering 'Dove', *a light pink English rose, forms a hedge along a rustic pathway, joined by lambs' ears (***Stachys byzantina***) and a pink* **Dianthus.**
(Pat and Stan Henry garden, Laurens, SC)

(opposite) **Two old-fashioned roses** *flank a simple path. The Moss rose 'Salet' is on the left and Bourbon 'Great Western' (right). They're beautifully accented with the dark, red-bronzy leaves of coral bells (***Heuchera** spp.) and a Japanese barberry (***Berberis thunbergii***).*
(Sabrina and Freeland Tanner garden, Yountville, CA)

The perfect little rosebuds of 'Climbing Cécile Brünner' open to puffy flowers that fade to white. Here they grace the weathered, front-porch steps of a home. *(Catherine Corison garden, St. Helena, CA)*

Highlight Steps for Safety

Negotiating steps can be tricky, so we tend to watch where our foot falls as we reach them. Bright Miniature roses—especially white ones such as white 'Popcorn', 'Snowball', and 'Yorkshire Sunblaze'—are easily seen at dusk and can help mark the location of steps. Plant them right beside the steps so they spill over the edge just a bit, but take care not to let them ramble so far as to become a hazard.

Because steps cut into a slope, Ground Cover roses can dress up the area and help prevent erosion. Good Ground Cover roses include 'Red Cascade', a rich red repeat bloomer, and 'Snow Carpet', a white rose. Both are hardy to Zone 5. 'Sea Foam' is an even hardier white Ground Cover rose. It is hardy to Zone 4, along with the 'Flower Carpet' series—disease-resistant roses that come in red, apple-blossom pink, and white. Mix these roses with dwarf forms of evergreens like mugo pine (*Pinus mugo*), blue spruce (*Picea pungens* f. *glauca*), juniper (*Juniperus procumbens*), and *Cotoneaster*. It's also a nice idea to place an archway at the top or bottom of the steps and grow a rose over it. Entering a set of steps through a rose-covered arch makes climbing the steps a special event.

Drape Your Windows in Roses

Growing roses around windows makes a wonderful impression. The window, seen from outside, is dressed in finery. And the world, seen through the window, is encircled with roses. When choosing roses to train up to and around a window, consider their fragrance—how sweet when breezes entering the house carry their scent. You might also consider security and think of roses' wicked thorns as a plus—unless you lose your keys and have to enter through the window yourself. Above all, looks are paramount. Do you want to make a bold impression or a subtle statement? The stronger the color, the louder the statement. To my mind, a subtle statement is often more appropriate around windows. Pastel roses, especially blush pinks, seem to have an affinity for bedroom windows, while soft yellow roses give an echo of sunshine under or around living-room windows.

Three different roses spring up from the foundation to grace this brick wall and window. The clusters of small, single, pink roses belong to the Hybrid Musk 'Ballerina'. The bright pink Hybrid Tea is 'Louise Estes'. The Modern Climber 'Pierre de Ronsard' scampers up the wall. *(Anna Davis garden, Atlanta, GA)*

'Climbing Cécile Brünner' is a choice that leaps to mind because it is such a common and popular rose. However, Climbers with larger flowers such as the pink 'Constance Spry' and 'New Dawn', white 'Climbing Iceberg' and 'Alberic Barbier', red 'Dublin Bay' and 'Henry Kelsey', and yellow 'Climbing Allgold' and 'Climbing Arthur Bell' make more memorable statements around windows.

Coordinate Curtains and Roses

The effect of roses framing a window is a lovely one. And it can be enhanced, especially when viewed from inside the house, when the window curtains are carefully color-coordinated with the roses. Solid-colored fabric that echo the roses outside are effective, but so are print curtains that look as much like the roses as possible, so that the view from the window continues into the house. If you're starting from scratch, choose the fabric first; then choose the roses.

Harmonize Colors

Overall, natural materials like stone, brick, and wood are most accepting of any color rose. With painted walls and window trim, careful color harmony pays big dividends, especially as the colors become more saturated. Natural colors and pastel greens make fine backdrops for any rose, especially when dark green rose foliage accompanies them. As a general rule, select a flower color that is close to that of the wall but richer or more saturated in hue. Train rich red roses onto a pale pink stucco wall, for instance, or pale apricot or peachy roses on a yellow-orange wall. Make sure the rose color, not the wall color, is the dominant visual feature. Since wall color is the permanent factor here, choose a rose that will stand out against the wall color. That's a lot easier than painting your house to match a rose.

Brick walls are ideal for yellow, orange, mauve, or pink roses. I still recall the stunning sight of a Lady Banks rose sprawling and billowing its mounds of pale yellow flowers over an aged-brick wall at Filoli Gardens, south of San Francisco, when I think of the perfect combination of rose and wall color. Some reds can get lost against the brick unless, like 'Don Juan' or 'Mr. Lincoln', they have especially rich colors—so match carefully.

Contrasting combinations will work, too. A blue doorway surrounded by the pale pink flowers of 'New Dawn' creates a superb composition, and a yellow rose against a pale blue wall is a cheery sight. If you've made friends at a local rose nursery, you might ask to take home a bunch of roses blooming in their pots to see which colors work best against your backgrounds, and then return the rest.

The rich, periwinkle-blue *paint of the shutters and window box contrasts with the creamy-yellow flowers of a Lady Banks rose (R. banksiae 'Lutea'). Rather than distract, the contrast enhances the Lady Banks' modest color and helps display its sensuous form.*

When growing roses up around windows, select a flower color that is close to that of the wall, but richer or more saturated in hue.

The apricot buds, *warm-pink new flowers, and whitish fading flowers of 'Abraham Darby' strike a color harmony with a pale stucco wall.*

Training Roses around Windows

Imagine how stark this window would look without the Climbing Polyantha 'Phyllis Bide' adding its crown of roses. Notice that a white clematis is sprinkling its big flowers among the roses. *(Dotty and Jim Walters garden, Healdsburg, CA)*

Most roses that are vigorous enough to grow up a wall and surround a window are also vigorous enough to bury the window in canes and foliage, so you'll need to keep them in check. Try thinking of them as espaliers—that is, they must display themselves two-dimensionally in space.

Get Them Off to a Good Start

In the first year, allow them to grow pretty much as they will, selecting an especially long, strong cane and positioning it up the wall. During the dormant season, trim off all the canes except the one you've chosen. In spring, the first growth will usually be at the tip of the cane, where most of the growth hormones are located. This new growth should be lengthy enough to train around a window. If it isn't, trim back some of the bushy growth closest to the roots so that the plant puts more energy into the growing tip. Growth from the leaf axils along the stems will usually be shorter and, if they received enough sunshine, very floriferous. In subsequent years, either trim away canes that are growing straight out from the wall or train them to the wall.

Roses that are vigorous enough to reach the second story usually want room to expand horizontally as well as vertically. As they grow up to the second floor, some canes will tumble out and twirl down, making showers and waterfalls of roses—a very pleasing effect—so give these rampant growers plenty of room to sprawl.

When you plant roses to ascend a wall and reach a window, place them a good 2 feet from the foundation so their roots can expand in all directions. Also be aware that cement walls and foundations will tend to raise the pH of

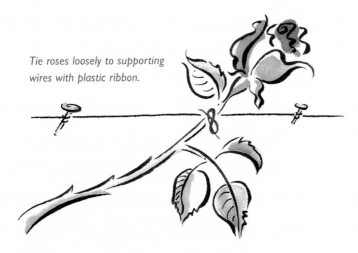

Tie roses loosely to supporting wires with plastic ribbon.

the soil near to them, so it's a good idea to use plenty of compost (which usually has the slightly acid pH that roses prefer) in the planting hole and as a topdressing every year.

Provide a Sturdy Support System

Roses are grown on wires that are attached to lag bolts in stone, brick, and masonry walls, or to long screws with eye hooks in frame houses. If you have aluminum siding, drill holes, secure the screws or eye hooks, and then fill around the holes with weatherproof sealant.

A horizontal wire held about 3 inches away from the wall will allow you to tie the elongating canes to the wire easily. Using soft, green, plastic ribbon (available at garden centers), tie the canes to the outside of the wire; don't run them between the wire and the wall. On the way up the wall, the wires may need to be strung every 3 or 4 feet, with a horizontal length of about 6 feet or so. Most Climbing roses will not get much wider than that. When the roses reach the top of the window, run a wire about 2 feet above the top of the window casing and train the growth along it. When it reaches the other side of the window, you can then let it hang down and grow as it pleases, or attach more horizontal wire to confine it.

Another way to train roses up a wall to a window is to run wires vertically from an earth anchor (set near the plant, about 2 feet from the wall) up the wall to either eye hooks set into the wall, or to hooks set into the eaves of the roof. The wires will then form a widening framework as they ascend. However, support is not nearly as strong as with horizontal wires. You can also grow roses on a trellis held well away from the wall by 3-inch spacers. Just make sure the roses don't grow between the trellising and the wall, where they invite mildews and rots, and are very hard to reach when pruning.

Splay roses along wire or trellis scaffolding so that they receive plenty of sunlight.

A vigorous Climber *reaches a second-story window at Sissinghurst. The dark red flowers harmonize with the lighter-colored brick, and complement the lilac-blue puffs of the shrubby California lilac (Ceanothus spp.) below.*
(Sissinghurst Castle, Kent, England)

Reaching the Second Story

Where there's a balcony at the second story, it may be possible to grow a less vigorous rose in a large container and train it up and over a second-story window. Floribundas and Grandifloras are ideal for this purpose, as you can tie some canes up and over the window and let others spill over the edge. If they don't have enough weight to do this themselves, it's easy enough to tie a small weight of some inconspicuous sort (such as a lug-nut or fishing-line weight) to a cane about two thirds of the way out, which will help it spill gracefully over the edge. You certainly aren't limited to Modern roses, however. The same technique of weighting canes can be used with a Bourbon like 'Souvenir de la Malmaison', an Alba like 'Félicité Parmentier', or a strongly perfumed Damask like 'Rose de Rescht'. For continuous bloom, though, David Austin's English roses, Climbing Miniatures like 'Red Cascade', or Floribundas can't be beat.

Some exceptionally vigorous Climbers and Ramblers—most notably some of the light-flowered varieties like 'Dundee Rambler', 'La Mortola', 'Rambling Rector', 'Seagull', and 'Wedding Day', along with some vigorous species like *R. banksiae*, *R. foetida*, *R. helenae*, *R. moschata*, *R. mulliganii*, *R. phoenicia*, and *R. rubus*—may end up clambering onto the roof. It's a tempting idea to let them ramble up there, as they will be visually imposing, soften the outlines of the house, and may help cool the attic on hot summer afternoons. But remember that fall will come and they will go dormant, so gutters should have good leaf screens over them. They'll also be out of reach for easy pruning. And unless they are tied firmly up there, they could, when their weight becomes sufficient, slide off the roof and pull everything down with them.

Choice Roses
for Framing Windows

Roses for first-story windows:

'Climbing Iceberg' ✿ Beautifully formed white flowers are held, Floribunda-style, in large trusses against attractive, dark green foliage in spring. It is disease resistant. Zone 5.

'Constance Spry' ✿ This arching English rose has the lovely, clear pink color of 'Wife of Bath' and something of its face-powder scent. The once-blooming flowers are double in the style of Old Garden roses, and the canes carry gray-green foliage. Zone 4.

'New Dawn' ✿ This looks much like 'Dr. W. Van Fleet', of which it is a sport, except that it is shorter and continues flowering after its summer flush. Same delightful perfume, too. Zone 5.

'Pink Perpetue' ✿ An offspring of 'New Dawn', but with darker, more intense pink flowers, it produces masses of semidouble blossoms in clusters through the summer. Zone 5.

'Sympathie' ✿ This is a rich red rose with a light fragrance and fully double blossoms that appear continuously throughout summer. Zone 5.

'Constance Spry'

Roses for second-story windows:

'Dr. W. Van Fleet' ✿ This rose has blush-pink, scented flowers. It's vigorous and thorny, but blooms just once in the summer. Zone 4.

'Mermaid' ✿ This rose produces a continuous display of single blossoms with light yellow petals and golden centers, and carries a pretty scent. It needs sturdy support to grow on a wall, but is worth the trouble. Zone 6.

'Evangeline' ✿ Dark green foliage provides a nice backdrop for clusters of small, faintly scented, single flowers whose pink petals turn white toward the center, and are ringed by a cluster of golden stamens. Blooms late in the season. Zone 4.

'Francois Juranville' ✿ This rose has a clean, fruity scent, and its once-blooming, slightly fluted, blush-pink flowers, which are born in loose, open clusters, look more like mums than roses. Zone 5.

'Mme. Caroline Testout' ✿ This is a floriferous and sometimes repeat-blooming Hybrid Tea touting large, round, pink flowers with curled edges. It is lightly scented. Zone 6.

Two climbing roses—*Climbing Tea 'Souvenir de Mme. Léonie Viennot' and Climbing Hybrid Tea 'Lady Waterlow'—have all but inundated this home's enclosed porch roof. They're pretty on a roof, but require frequent pruning to keep them from getting out of hand.* (Nancy Duncan garden, Charlotte, NC)

Perk Up Decks, Porches, and Patios

Porches, verandas, and deck railings are ready-made scaffolding for beautiful roses. In fact, porch posts are among the best supports for climbing roses. The porch on the south side of my house has a gorgeous specimen of 'Red Cascade', a Climbing Miniature that throws out sprays of small, bright red flowers all season—once it gets going in late June. 'Kathleen Harrop' is a Climbing Bourbon with a lot of good characteristics for the porch post: It's a continuous bloomer, very fragrant, and will take some shade.

Twining Up Posts

Roses are usually kept to the vertical porch posts where they can be seen and smelled, but are out of harm's way. It's certainly possible to train them along the horizontal porch railings, but then the railings are taken out of use as places for people to place their hands or to lean against.

Because porches are covered with roofs, roses grown under eaves simply don't get enough sun to flower dependably, but if your porch has a south-west exposure and you can train the roses along the edge of the roof like a valance, this is a beautiful way to grow vigorous Climbers. Roses can be also grown up the support posts of decks. But just as with porches, they are not the best choices for training along deck railings because of their prickly thorns.

Two Climbing Floribundas worthy of consideration are the white 'Climbing Iceberg' and the yellow 'Climbing Allgold', although these only flower in summer. Modern Climbing roses offer a wide choice for continuous-flowering selections: 'Altissimo', 'Dublin Bay', 'Etude', 'Parade', 'Pink Perpetue', and 'White Cockade' all produce wave after wave of bloom. They'll do best if either wound around the porch post or twisted

Roses are usually kept to the vertical porch posts where they can be seen and smelled but are out of harm's way.

A Rosy Valance

Trim the edge of your porch roof with any of the roses recommended for growing up and around second-story windows. Buy two and train them up the posts at each end of your porch, allowing them to grow toward each other across the eave and overlap when they meet. Keep the roses cut back to two or three main canes, and prune the flowering side shoots to about 6 inches or two or three buds each year. The view *from* your porch will be enhanced by this valance of roses, as will the view *of* your porch.

'Phyllis Bide', *a Climbing Polyantha, twirls its relatively thorn-free canes up a porch post in a luscious display of its yellow, cream, and pink, lightly fragrant blossoms.* (Joy Wolff garden, Healdsburg, CA)

back and forth on the sunny side of the post. My favorite climbing rose for porches, however, is 'New Dawn'. This rose has an easily trainable habit, continuous bloom of soft pink roses, and a fine scent. Keep 'New Dawn' deadheaded for best appearance and to stimulate bloom.

Wrap with a Floral Skirt

A good way to use roses around both porches and decks is to create a floral skirt along its edge. As with any foundation planting, simply edging the deck or porch with variously colored roses isn't as effective as planting them in groups, with spaces between the groups for other plants. At each corner of your deck or porch, consider planting a large shrub rose flanked by two or three smaller roses. Because you are often looking down on these roses from the deck or porch, Hybrid Teas might be a good choice because they hold their blooms upright, but any roses suitable for foundation plantings are appropriate.

If there are no gutters on the edge of your porch roof, plant the roses beyond the drip line so that they don't take the heavy wash of roof runoff from summer cloudbursts. In all cases, plant them at least 2 feet from the edge of the porch so that both the roots and foliage have room to grow. And keep in mind that if they are planted beneath a roof eave, they will probably need supplemental irrigation.

'Weller Bourbon', *a large, deep pink Bourbon, creates an exciting display as it finds its way out of a bed of fleabane (Erigeron karvinskianus) onto a white porch. Judicious pruning of the shrubby Bourbon gives it the shape of a loose climber.* (Joy Wolff garden, Healdsburg, CA)

A Colorful Splash around Patios

Patio roses were developed specifically for low edging and mixed borders around patios, courtyards, and terraces. Patio roses are slightly taller and shrubbier than Miniature roses, usually with somewhat larger flowers. At 1½ to 2 feet tall, they won't obscure the view beyond the patio, but will add color and define the edge. Looking toward the house, their color should harmonize with the building materials, and looking away from the house, associate with roses and other plants in the landscape.

Most Patio roses are continuous bloomers, so they remain colorful through the growing season. My favorite is probably 'Sweet Dreams', with blush-apricot and peach blooms on 18-inch plants. There are dozens of Patio roses to choose from, many bred by the famous house of McGredy in New Zealand. Also, the Poulsen rose breeders of Denmark have come up with a new range of hardy, low-maintenance, and disease-resistant continuous bloomers perfect for either edging or spreading a

*Two white **Floribunda** 'Iceberg' roses grown as standards grace the steps leading from one level of a patio to the other. In the foreground, flanking a bench, two 'Prospero' Austin roses enjoy life in well-fertilized containers. David Austin says of 'Prospero' that "their form is faultless...of the very highest old rose perfection. There is also a strong old rose fragrance."* (Carol Brewer garden, El Cajon, CA)

Container-grown roses can punctuate the garden, creating the perfect focal point in unexpected places.

The sturdy, simple lines of a eucalyptus tree are contrasted in this patio by an underplanting of fleabane (Erigeron karvinskianus) and 'Ballerina', a Hybrid Musk with small, single, pink flowers with white centers. (Diane and Johnathan Spieler garden, Lafayette, CA)

carpet of bloom here and there. Some of their nicest selections are the yellow 'Aspen', dark peach 'Augusta', and bright red 'Napa Valley'.

Miniature roses are useful around patios in small containers, in window boxes that face the patio, and even in hanging baskets that are low enough for the roses to be seen. If your patio is raised slightly above ground level, an edging of roses gives a visual clue that a step is required. An excellent way to tie the patio into the surrounding lawn or garden is to place several long planters with Miniatures on the edge of the patio, and then place Patio roses behind them in pots, planters, or the soil at the edge of the patio. These, in turn, can be backed by groupings of taller Shrub roses, creating a tiered effect and softening the hard edges of the patio by interrupting them. The roses, then, will ease the transition from patio tile or stone to the greenery beyond.

Suitable for Containers

Visiting a friend's house in Long Island, New York, I noticed a large urn set at one end of his patio planted with a rose that spilled out and down over the edges in a most attractive way. I should have recognized its pink flowers as 'The Fairy', a Polyantha, immediately, but had to ask him its name because its slender stems drooped so fetchingly over the edges of the urn. He noticed my surprise when he told me its name, and then showed me why it drooped so nicely—he'd tied large metal hex nuts under the branch tips to weigh them down. He said that after a season, the branches would stay that way, and he'd have to prune just the few stems that started growing straight up in future years.

Container-grown roses can punctuate the garden, creating the perfect focal point in unexpected places. Place a favorite specimen rose in a beautiful container at the end of a walkway, at a bend in a path or in a mixed border—anywhere you wish to draw the eye.

Patio Planting Pockets

When laying a patio or terrace, leave out several randomly spaced tiles, bricks, pavers, or flagstones so that the underlying soil is exposed. Or, if you are pouring a concrete patio, set a few randomly spaced #10 aluminum cans (or any cylinder about 8 inches in diameter) on the soil before you pour the slab, and remove them once the concrete has set. Improve the soil in these spaces and put in a few favorite plants. Patio roses, Ground Cover roses, and procumbent Shrub roses (such as pink 'Flower Carpet', white 'Kent', or red 'Red Bells') are all suitable for growing in planting pockets and, as they fill in, will look like they are growing right out of the patio. Small ornamental grasses and succulents are also good choices for these spaces. So that they don't become a hazard, it's usually best to keep these planting pockets close to the edges of your patio or terrace.

Remove bricks or pavers and amend the soil beneath to create planting pockets in patios.

Small Varieties Suit Containers

Near my house are two white pillars flanking the roadway. The large depression in the top of each pillar is planted with a Lady Banks rose, whose long canes come spilling up and out in a very pretty effect. While you can grow large roses like this Lady Banks in large containers, the easiest roses to grow in containers are the smallest—the Miniature and Patio roses. Urns, pots, and wooden planters with these diminutive roses, placed at the corners and edges of patios and terraces, help soften the

Rose standards are wonderful
flanking a doorway or
placed along paths.

This gardener had the brilliant idea of using
a container of the Floribunda 'Iceberg' in
front of two 'Iceberg' standards to add life
to a row of evergreen foundation shrubs.
(Ann Otterson garden, La Jolla, CA)

lines of the hardscaping and bring some of the garden's color and foliage toward the house. Small rose standards (upright roses clipped into lollipop shapes) in square, squat boxes are excellent for this purpose.

Rose standards are especially wonderful flanking a doorway or placed along paths. The containers, as well as the roses, can lend artistry to the pathway. Consider bordering a path with mixed shrubs and flowering plants, and set rose standards behind them. A rich pink or red standard behind blue-flowered perennials like Russian sage (*Perovskia atriplicifolia*) or blue mist shrub (*Caryopteris* × *clandonensis*) is a stunning sight. If the roses begin to look shabby or have stopped flowering for the season, they can simply be moved away.

Spruce Up Window Boxes

Miniature roses are especially suited to grow in window boxes. They can be pretty grown by themselves, but I think they look even better when mixed with small container plants such as pot marigold (*Calendula officinalis*), dusty miller (*Senecio cineraria*), evergreen candytuft (*Iberis sempervirens*), or nasturtium (*Tropaeolum majus*). If you have a sunny wall appropriate for window boxes, consider planting several Miniature roses, which will grow from 1 to 1½ feet tall, and accompanying them with trailing plants. One of the prettiest trailers is Dittany of Crete (*Origanum dictamnus*), which hangs its graceful stems over the edge and produces dusky rose-purple, hoplike seed heads. *Diascia* 'Ruby Field' is another stunner for the window box. Although it's a perennial, treat it like an annual in Zones 7 and colder. Johnny jump-ups (*Viola tricolor*) are favorite companions for miniature roses, as is *Sedum sieboldii*, a trailing succulent with dusty pink flowers in autumn. From *Alyssum* to *Zinnia*, there are dozens of great companions for Miniature roses in window boxes.

Most Miniatures require full sun, or at least four to six hours of direct sun a day, which means you'll need to site them on a sunny, south-facing wall. One of the few that will bloom in shady conditions is 'Anna Ford', of English provenance, with orange and yellow flowers. And as for their care, simply make sure they get plenty of water (daily in hot or dry climates) and regular fertilizer, and refresh the soil every three years. When growing roses in containers and window boxes, keep in mind that

The raggedy pink, *cream, and yellow petals of the Climbing Polyantha 'Phyllis Bide' dance around a container planted with the pure pink petals of the Procumbent Shrub rose 'Queen Mother', which is just starting to bloom.*

Wall Off a Dining Area

To set off an area of the patio or deck for dining or seating, place a long container planted with Patio or Miniature roses so that it defines an enclosure much in the way that a wall would define a room in your home. Fill this new outdoor "room" with chaise longues or a table, umbrella, and chairs. Give careful thought to the composition of both the patio or deck area and the view beyond. Place the furniture so that you get a nice view out into the garden. Add some containers of roses to enhance the space but not in a position where they would block your view. And coordinate the colors of the roses with your outdoor furniture, other deck or patio plantings, and the garden beyond.

the conditions for plants are more extreme than if they are grown in the ground. In hot climates, scorching summer sun can heat the soil in pots to a level that can damage plants, and in cool climates, winter temperatures can make potted roses feel a zone or two colder. So in summer, water your containers frequently and consider massing several pots together for a moderating effect or place them where they get shade from the hottest afternoon sun. Wooden window boxes left natural or painted

light colors will reflect the heat of the sun. In winter, move your pots and window boxes to a protected spot. You'll also need to refresh the soil each year. Simply remove the roses from the containers, retaining as much of the root ball and attached soil as you can, and set them aside. Mix well-made compost with some sand and either vermiculite or perlite, and repot the roses in the new soil.

Dressing Up a Mailbox

Those of us with mailboxes in the apartment foyer or a post office box are out of luck, but those with a real rural mailbox sitting atop a post have the perfect place for a small, twining rose. It not only greets the mail carrier with its pretty look, it pleases everyone who passes by. Just make sure it's not so thorny or overgrown that opening the mailbox becomes a challenge.

Of the hundreds of appropriate roses to choose from, I like 'Ballerina', a well-behaved Hybrid Musk with dainty, pink and white blossoms all summer long. It's a 4-foot shrub that can be easily trained around a mailbox or small lamppost. The trick is to keep it to three or four stems and train them around the post in opposite directions. Procumbent Shrub Roses, usually used as ground covers, can be treated the same way. 'Sea Foam' is a repeat-blooming, creamy-white variety of Ground Cover rose whose 4-foot stems will take to a post. A couple of Polyanthas planted on either side of a post can make a vivid impression with continuously produced sprays of lovely small roses. My favorite is 'The Fairy', a pink charmer with 2- to 3-foot stems for training. Mailbox posts, lampposts, and small pillars trained with twining roses all announce that a lover of roses lives at this location. Even in a very rural situation, a display of roses by the road makes a fine transition onto the property.

Mailboxes can be stark little objects, except when they're paired with a rose as beautiful as the Austin 'Kathryn Morley', whose clear pink, prettily cupped, fragrant roses will bloom all summer. (Catherine Corison garden, St. Helena, CA)

When planting roses farther from the house, consider drought-tolerant roses—those that, while they don't really like drought, can get by on usual summer rainfall east of the Mississippi, and require only minimal irrigation in the west. Some of the most drought-tolerant roses are the Albas, Multiflora Hybrids, *R. rugosa* hybrids and Modern Shrub roses, along with many of the new, low-maintenance, landscape roses like the 'Carefree' series.

Add a Few Companions

You can enhance rose-adorned posts and pillars by growing them with small shrubs and perennials. Good companion shrubs might include dwarf azalea (*Rhododendron* spp.), false cypress (*Chamaecyparis* spp.), *Pittosporum*, sweet box (*Sarcococca* spp.), and mugo pine (*Pinus mugo*). Hardy geraniums (*Geranium* spp.), catmint (*Nepeta* spp.), and *Artemisia* are classy perennials to join them, as are other twining vines like *Clematis* (always the perfect choice with roses), morning glories (*Ipomoea* spp.), black-eyed Susan vine (*Thunbergia alata*), the cup-and-saucer vine (*Cobaea scandens*), and sweet peas (*Lathyrus odoratus*). And if you live in Zone 10, by all means plant the Chilean bellflower (*Lapageria rosea*) on a tall post. Associate its gorgeous rosy-red, waxy bells with white or light pink, continuous-blooming Climbing roses for an outstanding display.

In this mixed planting around a lamppost and gate arbor, 'Gold Flame' honeysuckle (*Lonicera heckrottii 'Gold Flame'*) takes top position over the arbor while the Floribunda 'Permanent Wave' adds a strong red base to the composition. (*Orene Horton garden, Columbia, SC*)

Chapter 4

In Mixed Plantings

F OR MORE THAN A CENTURY, it has been common practice to grow roses in beds created for them exclusively, whether in formal or informal arrangement. Paths were left through and around these beds so that gardeners could spray for insects, trim off infected leaves, deadhead spent flowers, and pull any weeds that dared grow there. The ground under the plants was kept bare or sometimes mulched. Beds were thus horticultural art galleries, where the best new introductions could be admired, and maintenance could be handled most easily.

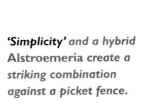

'Simplicity' and a hybrid Alstroemeria *create a striking combination against a picket fence.*

Annuals make good fillers among roses and perennials in borders. Here, Johnny jump-ups (Viola tricolor) provide a colorful accent for the Floribunda 'Pleasure'. (Sally Cooper garden, Charlotte, NC)

Yet it is the very proximity of so many roses in one place that creates conditions conducive to the spread of diseases like mildews, rots, black spot, rust, and anthracnose, and where insects like thrips, mites, aphids, and chafers are presented with a banquet of their favorite hosts. I once asked a commercial rose grower who had a large number of acres planted in Hybrid Teas how he kept them looking so good. "Spray, spray, and spray some more," he said. The problem with spraying so often is that it's a drastic measure. It takes many trips to the garden with a sprayer to keep the plants protected. Chemicals have to be carefully prepared. Protection needs to be worn. The sprayer needs to be cleaned out in a way that residue doesn't contaminate the water supply. And sprays harm the delicate balance of life in a garden.

Fortunately, the era of exclusive focus on the segregated rose garden is fast disappearing. Gardeners are rediscovering the beauty of many of the species roses and old-fashioned roses, and hybridizers are introducing new roses that are hardier, more resistant to pests and diseases, and require less maintenance. It's these new roses, in particular, that are opening new opportunities for adding color to mixed plantings. Many roses are perfectly at home with flowering shrubs and perennials rather than being segregated into their own beds. Many roses have slender stems and a twining habit, which makes them perfect for growing into large shrubs and small trees—the roses find their way up through the structure of the woody plants and reach the sunlight between their branches, like flowers pleated into a woman's hair. And some roses are perfect for adding a splash of color to orchards, vegetable gardens, and vineyards.

An Anchor for Beds and Borders

Borders and island beds often highlight the garden, featuring a colorful and textural mix of annuals, perennials, ornamental grasses, and flowering shrubs. You may also find small trees, a few evergreen shrubs, annuals, and seasonal bulbs. Many roses are good companions and can anchor

Choice Roses
for Pleasing Habit and Shape

'Abraham Darby' ✿ A vigorous grower with tall, thorny, arching stems and shiny, dark green leaves. This fragrant, repeat-blooming English rose has warm pink, old-fashioned flowers. Zone 5.

'Alba Semi-plena' ✿ This graceful, old Alba has a soft sweep of 6- to 8-foot stems and fragrant, white flowers that bloom once a year. Zone 3.

'Bonica' ✿ This rose grows wider than tall, and is an excellent specimen in the garden or container. Frilly, double flowers are produced all summer. It's one of the prettiest Shrub roses. Zone 4.

'The Fairy' ✿ At only 2 feet tall, this continuous-blooming Polyantha spreads oodles of luscious, pink flowers over stems that cover a 4- to 5-foot radius. Zone 5.

'Félicité et Perpétue' ✿ One of the prettiest roses to grow up walls. It has mildly scented, double, white flowers touched with pink and blooms once a year. Zone 6.

'Fru Dagmar Hastrup' ✿ A compact *R. rugosa* hybrid that is beautiful enough to make a specimen in any garden. Carries single, clear pink roses all summer and fall. Zone 2.

'Gruss an Aachen' ✿ It grows to only 2 feet with slender, prettily arranged stems, excellent foliage and soft, shell-pink blooms with peach highlights. It blooms continuously and carries a lovely fragrance. An exceptional, small Floribunda. Zone 5.

'Lavender Dream' ✿ A medium-sized Shrub rose with gracefully arching stems that carry clusters of semidouble, lavender-pink roses all summer. Zone 7.

'R. banksiae' ✿ The Lady Banks rose is tender, but where it grows, it makes an enormous display of long, slender canes covered with fine-leaved foliage and a profusion of tiny, soft yellow roses in early spring. Zone 8.

'Red Cascade' ✿ A lovely Climbing Miniature with long, pliable stems—perfect for growing up a porch, post, or pillar—with clusters of small, rich red roses all summer long. Zone 5.

R. banksiae 'Lutea'

'The Fairy'

beds and borders. Continuous-blooming roses can provide color throughout the growing season.

Designing for Impact and Access

The difference between a border and a bed is its location: A border has a backdrop such as a house, fence, or woods and is viewed from one side; an island bed floats in a sea of grass or is surrounded by paving and can be viewed from all sides.

Because they need attention throughout the season—even low-maintenance beds and borders need tidying up, deadheading, and perhaps a little spraying—don't make your beds so wide that you can't reach the center without stepping on plants or compacting your soil. For island beds, which can be accessed from all sides, this usually means a maximum width of about 8 feet, unless the beds have stepping-stones. For borders against a wall or fence, 4 feet is the limit unless you place a narrow path along the back of the border (which could double its width). If your border backs up to the woods, you might be able to make it wider than 4 feet by providing access through the woods.

Island beds display their roses best when they build up in height from the edge to a single peak near the center—but not right in dead center, which would feel too static. They might be edged with Miniature roses or broad-leaved perennials like lambs' ears (*Stachys byzantina*) or Berggarten sage (*Salvia officinalis* 'Berggarten'), then filled with taller, blowsy, small-flowered perennials such as colewort (*Crambe cordifolia*), baby's breath (*Gypsophila paniculata*), plume poppy (*Macleaya cordata*), which can be invasive if not confined), or clary sage (*Salvia sclarea*) and the upright spires of foxgloves (*Digitalis* spp.), queen of the prairie (*Filipendula rubra* 'Venusta'), nettle-leaved mullein (*Verbascum chaixii* f. *album*), spike speedwell (*Veronica spicata*), or *Delphinium*. And finally, toward the center of the bed, you'd find tall, lax Shrub roses, perhaps punctuated with a clump of feather reed grass (*Calamagrostis* × *acutiflora*

The pink Hybrid Musk 'Ballerina' anchors this border and is repeated throughout the garden. *(Susan and Ernie Collins garden, Woodside, CA)*

Beds and borders can be either geometrically shaped or free-formed, with deep dips and gentle curves.

Play Around with Pots

When designing a mixed border or island bed, leave the roses in their pots while you experiment with their placement. You may want a big splash of color by a large rock, a drift of soft-colored roses running down a gentle slope, or a large rose anchoring the back of a bed. If the roses are still in their pots, you can move them around until you get just the look you want. It's easiest to do this when the roses are blooming, but even roses without flowers will help you picture your garden. Once you've sited your roses, leave them in their pots while you set the pots of perennials or other plants around them. Once you're satisfied, start digging.

A wall of roses *provides a colorful backdrop for this evergreen parterre.* (Peter Newton garden, St. Helena, CA)

'Karl Foerster') or a large, leafy shrub like redtwig dogwood (*Cornus alba*) or smoke bush (*Cotinus coggyrigia*).

You may have heard that plants in borders should be arranged like school kids being assembled for a class photo, with the smallest plants in front, medium-sized plants in the middle, and the tallest plants in back. And in general, this is good practice if you want each plant to be seen. However, it is also about as exciting as a school picture. So don't be afraid to bring a pretty, fragrant, 5-foot Shrub rose close to the edge of the planting, where people's noses can get at it. Interrupt the regularity of the tiers here and there. If a rose or an ornamental grass of some stature hides something to one side or behind it, well, you'll just have to move a few steps to see back there. And if you're really clever, maybe you'll hide a treasured rose or other surprise behind that big fountain of grass.

In general, the taller the rose, the less frequently it should be used in the mixed bed or border. That's because roses tend to have such rich flower colors. A very large, tall rose will make such a forceful statement in a mixed planting that decorum may call for just a single specimen. Most roses mix best in the 2- to 3-foot zone, where many perennials are also found, and can be used more lavishly among the green growth there.

Shrubby Roses Suit Borders

The Floribundas are a wonderful class of roses for mixing. Their modest stature and continuous-blooming habit make them perfect for borders. Among the red Floribundas, 'Europeana', 'Sarabande', and 'Showbiz' are star performers. The best pinks include 'Betty Prior', 'Cherish', 'Gene Boerner', and 'Sweet Inspiration'. Among orange and apricot blends, 'Apricot Nectar' and 'Redgold' are stand-outs. And the yellow 'Sun Flare', white 'Iceberg', 'Ivory Fashion', mauve-lavender 'Angel Face' and 'Intrigue', have earned high awards from the All-America Rose Selections (AARS) committee.

Grandifloras, Polyanthas, and Modern Shrub roses are also top picks for the mixed border. Grandifloras grow 6 to 8 feet tall with large flowers on long clusters of stems. They get their vigorous, upright habit, and continuous-blooming, high-centered blossoms from the Hybrid Teas in their parentage. Because of their size and vigor, they function best in the background, where they can give a majestic sweep of color.

Polyanthas may be the perfect choice to plant in a low border above a wall, as they'll stay low-growing and spill over the wall with big sprays of small, 2-inch roses in colors like the coral of 'Margo Koster', the light pink of 'The Fairy', and the rich pink of 'China Doll'. (While 'Cécile Brunner' is a Polyantha and one of my favorites, it more closely resembles an upright shrub than a lax grower, heavy with trusses of roses, and so is better suited for midborder.)

Island beds display their roses best when they build up in height from the edge to a single peak near the center.

Plant in Odd-Numbered Groups

Most garden designers recommend planting perennials in groups of three, five, seven, or nine—depending on your overall garden size and the impact you'd like to make. It also makes sense to plant your roses in odd-numbered groups, as odd clusters have a much livelier look than even numbers, which tend to create a static symmetry. In an informal planting, feel free to change the varieties of roses from group to group. In formal gardens, repetition of the same rose creates continuity.

Though not arranged *as strictly as children in a school picture, staggered plantings like the Floribunda "Playgirl", Geranium 'Johnson's Blue', and lambs' ears (Stachys byzantina) shown here, are most effective.*
(Joanne Woodle garden, Peconic, NY)

A rose standard *serves as the centerpiece in a series of small, square island beds.*
(The Minikes Garden, designed by Carol Mercer, East Hampton, NY)

Choice Roses
among *David Austin's Rebloomers*

'Abraham Darby' ⚘ This large shrub grows to 5 feet, is very thorny, and displays double, apricot-to-yellow, sweetly fragrant flowers. Zone 5.

'Ambridge Rose' ⚘ A compact shrub about 3 feet tall and 2 feet wide that blooms all summer with abundant, very fragrant, large, double roses of peachy-apricot shading to blush-pink at the edges. Zone 5.

Modern Shrub roses have been bred for their cold hardiness, disease resistance, and attractive displays of flowers. Among the categories of Modern Shrub roses are the Hybrid Musks, English roses, Ground Cover roses, and Patio roses. Hybrid Musks function well in partial shade, so use them in a border near the woods, or along northeastern and northwestern exposures—just as long as they get at least four hours of sun a day.

David Austin's English roses are a miracle of rose breeding, giving us the look and fragrance of old-fashioned roses on trouble-free shrubs. And then there are Ground Cover roses like 'Flower Carpet' and 'Nozomi', Patio roses from Denmark, hardy roses bred especially for the northern states and Canada, and a handful of other roses whose parentage is, well, too complex for categorization. Among these are some of the world's

'Abraham Darby'

'Charles Rennie Mackintosh' Beautifully formed, double, lilac-pink, very fragrant flowers are produced all season on this 4-foot shrub. Zone 5.

'Charlotte' This bright, gold-yellow-white rose was bred from the popular yellow 'Graham Thomas'. It's a tall shrub that grows up to 6 feet, and blooms over a very long season— needing just a light pruning between flushes of flowers to keep the plant from becoming leggy. Zone 5.

'Dark Lady' This compact shrub features double, dark red, fragrant flowers. It is remontant rather than continuous blooming. Zone 5.

'Heritage' This classic Austin rose has double, light pink flowers on shrubs that make a good hedge if planted closely and kept lightly pruned. Zone 5.

'Jayne Austin' Although bred by David Austin, this rose is classified as a Modern Shrub rose. It features clusters of apricot-yellow flowers with darker eyes and strong fragrance. Zone 5.

'L. D. Braithwaite' This low, mounding rose carries crimson blossoms with a touch of cherry against gray-green foliage. It is ideal as a ground cover. Zone 5.

'The Prince' Plant several for a perfect 2-foot hedge with very fragrant, double, crimson blooms that fade to a purplish color. Zone 5.

favorite roses: 'Alchymist', the Meidiland hybrids, 'Bonica', 'Sally Holmes', and 'Sea Foam'. If you choose from among these roses for your beds and borders, you can't go wrong.

Perennials, the Perfect Companions

Roses, especially the continuous bloomers, are strong anchors for any bed border. Their success, however, often depends on those plants selected to play a supporting role. By far, the best companions for roses—beyond other roses—are perennials, grasses, and small shrubs. Herbaceous perennials can be used to hide the bare, stiff, thorny stems of many roses, and even the lax stems of certain roses. Blue, violet, lavender, and purple-flowered perennials are very useful with almost any rose color, from apricot and salmon to pink and red.

A Long-Season Color Display

Mixed borders of once-blooming roses, perennials, and shrubs remain mostly green as plants go in and out of flower. But continuous-blooming roses offer spots of color throughout the growing season around which the other colors change almost kaleidoscopically. Choose from among the Polyanthas, Floribundas, Grandifloras, and Modern Shrub roses like the Austins, Bucks, Kordseiis, Meidilands, and Meillands to create this season-long display of color in mixed borders.

Two Floribundas—*the red 'Trumpeter' and salmon 'Brass Band'—create a colorful composition in midborder with an assortment of tall flowers.*

Remember that most perennials are just foliage for most of the season, so coordinate with the foliage first. Besides dark to light greens and yellow-greens, perennials offer silver, blue-gray, gray-green, white, and dark-burgundy leaf colors. Fine leaves, like those of ferns or false bishop's weed (*Ammi majus*) contrast nicely with roses, even if they are similarly green. Perennials with foliage similar in size or shape to roses look best if the leaf colors of the plants can be varied. In other words, when the color is similar, vary the shape and size; when the shape and size are similar, vary the color.

Make sure your mixed plantings have some star performers for late in the year, when even continuous-blooming roses may be slowing down. While it's in the nature of most plants to bloom in the spring so they can set seed during the growing season, some plants, especially those suited to the warm zones, will bloom in the fall. You won't notice the chrysanthemums and asters during the height of summer, but they'll be a big part of the late garden.

Among the woody perennials and small shrubs, Scotch heather (*Calluna vulgaris*) blooms from August to October. In Zones 7 and warmer, the camellias (*Camellia* spp.) take up where roses leave off, often with similar white-, pink-, and red-colored flowers. A perfect choice with late-blooming pink or red roses is the blue mist shrub (*Caryopteris × clandonensis*) that carries deep blue, fringed flowers from August until frost—and grows only 2½ feet tall. In Zones 9 and 10, fuchsias (*Fuchsia* spp.) will bloom from June until frost. They often have strong colors, so mix them carefully with roses. However, I've seen a fuchsia with tall, graceful, arching stems dangle its bright, scarlet tubes among the pretty salmon-pink roses of 'Sexy Rexy', an excellent Floribunda, to great effect. Hydrangeas (*Hydrangea* spp.), St. John's wort (*Hypericum* spp.), bush cinquefoil (*Potentilla fruticosa*), chaste tree (*Vitex agnus-castus*), and Kashgar tamarisk (*Tamarix hispida*) all bloom from summer into fall.

Herbaceous perennials can be used to hide the bare, stiff, thorny stems of many roses.

Perennials with Colored Foliage

Perennials with colorful foliage help keep the garden interesting even when flowers are scarce. Silver, gray, and burgundy-hued leaves also make good blenders in the garden, and can be used to separate different color schemes. Here are some choice perennials with colorful foliage.

Lambs' ears

Silver or Gray Foliage

- *Artemisia stelleriana* 'Boughton Silver', *A.* 'Powis Castle'
- *Gypsophila paniculata* (baby's breath)
- *Senecio cineraria* (dusty miller)
- *Phlomis fruticosa* (Jerusalem sage)
- *Stachys byzantina* (lambs' ears)
- *Santolina chamaecyparissus* (lavender cotton)
- *Salvia argentea* (silver sage)
- *Achillea* 'Taygetea' (yarrow)
- *Thymus pseudolanuginosis* (woolly thyme)

Burgundy Foliage

- *Ajuga reptans* 'Burgundy Glow' (bugleweed)
- *Heuchera micrantha* var. *diversifolia* 'Palace Purple' (coral bells)
- *Athyrium niponicum* var. *pictum* (Japanese painted fern)
- *Salvia officinalis* 'Purpurascens' (purple sage)

Evergreens Add Winter Interest

Using evergreens in your border can provide structure, especially in winter when most plants are dormant and leafless. However, planted in groups, evergreens tend to grow dense and take over the composition, so use them sparingly. A single, cone-shaped juniper such as *J. communis* 'Sentinel' is good for anchoring a mixed planting, and I have seen a ground-hugging, silvery-blue juniper—probably one of the *Juniperus horizontalis* cultivars—form a very effective mat as it trailed down between rocks on a slope, with pink Meidiland Shrub roses set in small groups for color. Another exceptional planting I saw featured a camellia with its lower limbs pruned out to reveal the pretty, sinuous wood of the trunk. It was planted by a house where the eaves gave it a little shade, and fronted in full sun by a group of Floribunda roses.

Anticipate Changes

One of the joys of a bed or border is the serendipitous combination of colors, shapes, and textures that occur as plants mature. But as plants grow, beds often become overcrowded, and overcrowded beds become a jumble. Leaving ample space around your roses, perennials, and shrubs when you plant them will help prevent overcrowding, but the downside to this approach is that until plants mature, the garden may not look very full.

One solution is to plant roses, perennials, and shrubs based on their mature sizes, and fill the gaps with annuals that can be easily removed or left out as the garden grows. Another is more a matter of editing: Simply prune your roses and shrubs and divide your perennials as they outgrow their assigned spaces. You can also combine these planting strategies, or even fill in with small, continuous-blooming Modern Shrub roses, which can be easily dug up and moved to a new location after a few years.

Of course, even with good planning, you'll need to make changes in your beds and borders from time to time. There will be plants that make themselves all too happy in their new home; these should be removed

Favorite Perennial Companions

Catmint

Blue- and violet-flowered perennials make excellent companions for most roses. These cool colors associate beautifully with the reds, oranges, yellows, and pinks of roses. Use the shorter perennials as ground covers beneath Shrub roses and the taller ones as accents with Landscape roses. And don't be shy about trying your own favorite blue and violet flowers.

- *Aster* × *frikartii* (aster)
- *Campanula lactiflora, C. persicifolia* (bellflowers)
- *Echinops ritro* 'Taplow Blue' (small globe thistle)
- *Geranium* × *cantabrigiense* 'Biokovo' (hardy geranium)
- *Nepeta* × *faassenii* (catmint)
- *Perovskia atriplicifolia* (Russian sage)
- *Platycodon grandiflorus* (balloon flower)
- *Salvia officinalis* (culinary sage)
- *Salvia sclarea* (clary sage)
- *Salvia* × *sylvestris* 'Mainacht' (violet sage)
- *Thalictrum rochebruneanum* (meadow rue)
- *Verbena bonariensis* (tall verbena)
- *Verbena canadensis* 'Homestead Purple' (rose vervain)
- *Veronica* 'Sunny Border Blue' (speedwell)

before they force out other desirable plants. Some perennials, like thyme (*Thymus* spp.) and sage (*Salvia officinalis* spp.) tend to be shorter-lived than others and may need to be replaced. An unusually cold, wet winter or hot, dry summer may take its toll on even the toughest plants. Or perhaps some of your combinations didn't work out as expected. That's just the nature of gardening. Experimenting with new plants and moving existing plants around to create new combinations is part of what makes gardening so much fun.

Leaving ample space around your roses, perennials, and shrubs when you plant will help prevent overcrowding. Annuals can fill the gaps until these plants mature.

Pink and white fleabane (Erigeron karvin-skianus) carpets the ground beneath 'Weller Bourbon'. *(Joy Wolff garden, Healdsburg, CA)*

Cover Their Ankles with Ground Covers

No matter where roses are grown, they look their best with something other than bare soil beneath them. A ground cover of some sort—whether mulch, creeping plants or, ideally, a combination of the two—will suppress weeds, improve soil conditions, and provide an attractive setting for roses. I especially like adding a carpet of soft color beneath roses with small, mat-forming ground covers like woolly yarrow (*Achillea tomentosa*) or lambs' ears (*Stachys byzantina*). Succulents, such as hens and chicks (*Sempervivum* spp.) and sedums (*Sedum* spp.), contrast nicely with smaller roses, while leafy *Pachysandra procumbens*, Swan River and English daisies (*Brachyscome iberidifolia* and *Bellis perennis*), and sweet woodruff (*Galium odoratum*) make an interesting base for taller roses. Bushy ground covers like *Cotoneaster*, catmint (*Nepeta* spp.), and blue-flowered rosemary (*Rosmarinus officinalis* 'Tuscan Blue') also make good companions for tall, upright roses as they hide the roses' skinny legs.

Just be sure not to crowd your roses. Even when under-planted with ground covers, it's a good idea to leave some space next to the roses' stems covered only with mulch. This way, the plants won't be competing for moisture and nutrients, and you'll avoid creating an environment susceptible to fungal diseases.

One ground cover to avoid is ivy (*Hedera helix*). Once established, it will cover up roses and most other plants in a mixed bed. If you try to remove it, segments simply break off and grow back. Digging ivy out with a shovel is backbreaking work, and the few pieces you miss will soon re-root. (I know this from experience.)

Keep ground covers a foot or so from the base of roses so that they don't have to compete for nutrients. I like to give my

roses about 4 to 6 inches of nutritious compost, covered with pads of newspapers and topped with cocoa bean hulls or some other good-looking mulch.

Drape Trees with Colorful, Climbing Roses

A Climbing rose grown up into a large shrub or small tree makes a pretty picture in the orchard or backyard. In particular, Modern Climbing roses love the natural scaffolding of trees and have a way of twining their stems purposefully on their way up the trunk and into the canopy, and then allowing their stem tips to grow out and trail down in a pleasing way. The room they occupy aloft should not interfere with the tree's growth unless it is entirely mismatched—that is, if you are growing a monster rose like 'Rambling Rector' into a small English hawthorn (*Crataegus laevigata*).

Add a carpet of soft color beneath roses with small, mat-forming ground covers like woolly yarrow, lambs' ears, or succulents.

Trees with an open branching structure, like this peach (Prunus persica), offer the best scaffolding for roses like 'Climbing Old Blush'.

I once saw a chaste tree (*Vitex agnus-castus*) in full bloom here in the Bay Area of California, sending out its long, lilac-colored panicles. Twining through its center was a lovely cherry-pink, thornless, and fragrant rose which I believe was 'Zéphirine Drouhin'. What delightful companions they were! Other good roses that take well to climbing the natural scaffolding of small trees and shrubs include the blush-pink 'New Dawn', pink 'Pink Perpétue', rich red 'Parkdirektor Riggers', red 'Dublin Bay', and yellow 'Leverkusen'. All of these are well-behaved repeat bloomers. When matching trees and roses, choose Climbing roses whose extension will reach the mature height of the tree, and, if your tree is young, keep the rose pruned until the tree has a chance to grow, so they stay in balance.

Select Trees with Good Scaffolding

Small trees are usually placed behind shrubs in mixed plantings, especially in borders that front the large trees of woodlands. They can also be placed in small groupings—three is a nice number—throughout the landscape, with several roses adorning them. This can be a stunningly beautiful sight, especially when the lower limbs of the trees are pruned away and you can see patches of the landscape beyond through the trunks, while roses come tumbling from the foliage on top. Light pink, yellow, and white roses will almost glow against the dark or silvery leaves of many small trees. Suitable trees that are in foliage during rose season include the willow-leaved pear (*Pyrus salicifolia* 'Pendula'), cherry plum (*Prunus cerasifera*), olive (*Olea europaea*), star magnolia (*Magnolia stellata*), and serviceberries (*Amelanchier* spp.).

Almost any small tree grown in full sun can be used as a scaffolding and support for roses. Because of shape and habit, some are better than others. Look for those with an open branching structure that provides good air circu-

Training Roses into Trees

To train a rose into a tree, start with a small or moderately sized tree with an open canopy that grows in full sun.

About 3 or 4 feet from the trunk of the tree, dig a hole large enough to accommodate your Climbing rose. As you place the rose in the hole, tip it at a 45-degree angle toward the tree. Refill the hole with soil, and water well. Bamboo poles or other stakes can be placed alongside the rose to guide it to the tree. Tie the stakes loosely to the trunk so that they stay in place, and as the rose produces shoots, tie them loosely to the stakes. Once they reach beyond the first crotch of the tree, the shoots should be able to find their own way up the tree and out toward the sun.

Plant the rose about 3 ft. or 4 ft. from the tree at a 45° angle, and use a stake for support.

Thyme *is an attractive edger for borders. A good layer of mulch beneath 'Paradise' keeps ground covers from spreading all the way up to the rose stems.* *(Carol Mercer garden, East Hampton, NY)*

When matching trees and roses, choose Climbing roses whose extension will reach the mature height of the tree.

Look for trees with an open branching structure that provides good air circulation and access to sunlight.

'Champney's Pink Cluster', *a Noisette, scrambles through an oakleaf hydrangea (Hydrangea quercifolia), a deciduous shrub native to the southeastern United States that grows to 6 feet.* (Pat and Stan Henry garden, Laurens, SC)

lation and access to sunlight, and gives roses plenty of room to grow. Also, those with a few low branches are also nice, as they help get the roses off to a good start.

My favorite trees for growing with roses are the semidwarf apples. In spring, you get a blush of apple blossoms (with one of the sweetest, freshest fragrances of any plant, faint though it is) followed by tumbling roses, and later, luscious fruit. The semidwarf apples grow 12 to 14 feet tall—an excellent size to accommodate a Climbing rose. Both roses and apples are members of the *Rosaceae*, so if you spray the tree for apple scab or other pests and diseases, you will benefit the roses, too.

Beyond apples, my favorite flowering ornamental trees especially suited to supporting roses include the fringe tree (*Chionanthus virginicus*), which bears white panicles in June; the Japanese flowering dogwood (*Cornus kousa*), which sports white flowers in May and June; the Franklin tree (*Franklinia alatamaha*), which has white flowers late in the season; and the Carolina silverbell (*Halesia carolina*), whose strings of white bells hang beneath its branches in early May.

Some of the sturdier, large, deciduous shrubs that have an open habit suited to smaller Climbing roses are butterfly bush (*Buddleja alternifolia*), sweetshrub (*Calycanthus floridus*), redvein enkianthus (*Enkianthus campanulatus*), common pearlbush (*Exochorda racemosa*), winterberry (*Ilex verticillata*), beautybush (*Kolkwitzia amabilis*), hybrid mock orange (*Philadelphus* 'Snowgoose'), Van Houtte spirea (*Spiraea* × *vanhouttei*), common lilac (*Syringa vulgaris*), and many of the viburnums (*Viburnum* spp.).

Choose Loose, Open Evergreens

Broadleaved evergreen shrubs, such as *Photinia* × *fraseri*, leatherleaf viburnum (*Viburnum rhytidophyllum*), and the hollies (*Ilex* spp.), also offer good scaffolding for roses. You must, however, choose more carefully among the coniferous evergreens. The best conifers to use as scaffolding for roses are the open, angular ones, such as many of the pines (*Pinus* spp.). Modest-sized spruces (*Picea* spp.) can be used, too, but they need to be pruned to open up their interiors and prevent the formation of dense pyramids. Colorado blue spruces (especially *Picea pungens*

Roses with Annuals

Even continuous-blooming roses will have times during the growing season when they are out of flower. Keep color at their spots with annuals planted under and in front of the rosebushes. Annuals typically pump out color all season until frost cuts them down. Make sure the annuals' colors work with the roses.

Rosa glauca, *with its bluish foliage, makes a wonderful companion for this golden Hinoki cypress* **(Chamaecyparis obtusa 'Crippsii').** *(Joanne Woodle garden, Peconic, NY)*

'Hoopsii') respond well to this treatment. Prune so that there are several whorls of branches circling the tree and grow roses up into them. Depending on the size of the rose and the conifer, the pairing can be used as a focal point forward in the mixed planting or as a backdrop for lower-growing plants in front.

Let Vines Twine into Roses

While you often see Climbing roses growing up into small shrubs and trees, it's also possible to grow vines into sturdy Shrub roses. Some clematis, especially the smaller varieties, are fine companions for roses.

Clematis and roses, *like this 'Phyllis Bide', will always be classic companions.* *(Joy Wolff garden, Healdsburg, CA)*

Among the more modestly sized *Clematis* species that can be planted in the shade of a substantial rose bush—say, an 8-foot Grandiflora or *R. wichurana* hybrid like 'Alberic Barbier'—to grow up into its branches are the alpine clematis (*C. alpina* 'Pamela Jackman'), with nodding blue bells in May; downy clematis (*C. macropetala*), with lavender-blue, nodding bells in June; and scarlet clematis (*C. texensis*), with carmine-red, urn-shaped flowers from July to October.

Then there are the large-flowered, hybrid-clematis varieties most familiar to gardeners. Most grow 8 to 12 feet, and therefore need a large Climber or Rambler as a companion. Their lusciously colored, 4- to 8-inch blooms come in white, pink, lavender, blue, burgundy, magenta, and violet, often with a streaked with a darker shade. One of my favorites is 'Dr. Ruppel', which has eight ruffled, pink sepals streaked with dark carmine bars. It blooms in May and June, just in time to showcase itself with the 12-foot 'Sanders White Rambler' rose. All clematis like their roots firmly planted in the shade; their twisting vines will find the sun above.

Many other vines can also consort effectively with roses. There are the familiar annuals like sweet peas (*Lathyrus odorata*), morning glories (*Ipomoea* spp.), nasturtiums (*Tropaeolum* spp.), and black-eyed Susan vines (*Thunbergia alata*). In warmer climates, you have magnificent choices like *Clytostoma callistegioides*, Chilean bellflower (*Lapageria rosea*), and *Mandevilla* 'Alice DuPont'. And in colder regions, you can grow blue passionflower (*Passiflora caerulea*), hydrangea vine (*Schizophragma integrifolium*), and *Wisteria*.

Match Clematis to Rose

When growing clematis and roses together, pair the clematis to once-blooming roses that don't need a great deal of pruning so that the rose becomes scaffolding for the clematis. If you pair clematis with continuous-blooming roses that need severe pruning, the clematis will outrun the rose's new growth in the spring, creating a floppy mess.

Large-flowered, hybrid clematis need a large Climber or Rambler as a companion.

This small orchard is brightened by a colorful mix of roses and delphiniums.

Among Orchards, Vineyards, and Herb Gardens

Orchards with fruiting shrubs like black currants and gooseberries, brambles like raspberry and blackberry patches, and small fruit and nut trees are already a mixed planting, and can always use roses to add ornamental beauty. Perhaps you'd want to plant a hedge of roses along the edge of your orchard, or mix a few roses among the brambles—two gooseberries and an English rose grouped together form a trio all about the same size—a very thorny one at that. Roses can anchor the ends of a raspberry or blackberry patch, but be sure to confine the berries so their underground spreading roots, which can dive to 18 inches, don't choke out the roses. One way to do this is to bury a 2-foot-deep, plastic barrier in the ground at the end of the berry patch.

Roses have been grown in vineyards for ages. Because old roses were often susceptible to the same mildews that affect grape quality, and because roses show the appearance of mildew before the grapes, vineyard rows were often finished with roses at each end. The roses functioned like a canary in a coal mine—if the roses showed mildew, it was time to spray the grapes. Today, more sophisticated methods of assessing mildew problems are used. And yet, as a visit to any grape-growing region will reveal, roses still often finish the ends of vineyard rows, but now it's just for the beauty.

Roses also share a rich heritage with herbs. Whether culinary, medicinal, or ornamental in nature, herb gardens lend themselves to being dressed up by roses. The smaller herbs, such as thyme (*Thymus* spp.), Corsican mint (*Mentha requienii*), and chives (*Allium schoenoprasum*), make pretty under-plantings with taller Shrub roses. The blue-green leaves of rue (*Ruta graveolens*) and the silvery, gray-green leaves of *Artemisia* mix nicely with pink and red roses.

While many herbs have lovely flowers, most of the blossoms are small, if not inconspicuous. That's where a few roses, especially continuous-blooming types, can add splashes of season-long color to the herb garden. In formal herb gardens, roses anchor the garden in a way that few herbs can. And roses themselves aren't out of place as players in the fragrant herb garden, as their essential oils have been used in healing preparations since ancient times and their petals are common in potpourri blends. The volatile oils of herbs like rosemary (*Rosmarinus officinalis*), fleabane (*Erigeron* spp.), and *Artemisia* have an insect-repelling effect, too, which may help confuse or even deter rose pests in their search for a host. And a combination of roses and herbs from the garden will make a lovely arrangement in a vase on the dining-room table.

There's no reason why the vegetable garden ought to be devoted entirely to utilitarian crops. If there's a fence, there's scaffolding for Climbing and Rambling roses. In my garden, a gorgeous 'Abraham Darby' English rose greets me with beautifully shaped, quartered, lovely salmon-pink, and extremely fragrant flowers when I enter the gate. You can always find a spot for a pretty little Shrub rose among the cucumbers and the peppers.

Roses can anchor the ends of a raspberry or blackberry patch, but be sure to confine the roots of the berries so they don't choke out the roses.

Sometimes roses mingle among themselves, like 'Rosy Cushion', a dense Shrub rose, and 'New Dawn', a vigorous Climber.

Floribundas *are magnificent performers in the landscape, as white 'Iceberg' and pink 'Bonica' prove. Iceplant (Delosperma aberdeenense) carpets the ground between them with intense color.* (Marjorie McNair garden, La Jolla, CA)

Chapter 5

Throughout the Landscape

P EOPLE LOVE ROSES for their decorative and aesthetic qualities, but the uses of roses go far beyond their beauty. Roses can turn a large, open space into discreet areas for thematic plantings—rose hedges, for instance, that mark off spring bulb beds that are followed by long-blooming perennials. One of today's favorite ideas for landscaping is the creation of outdoor rooms where folks can get out of the house and enjoy a bit of al fresco living. When roses are at hand, especially when they form one or more of the "walls," their beauty and fragrance is one of the bonuses they add to these rooms.

Roses placed along the woods' edge, around ponds, and beside streams help create an ideal habitat for wildlife—providing food, shelter, and nesting sites.

Wherever there's structure in the landscape, there's a place for roses. The Modern Climbing rose 'Alchymist' decorates this rustic fence with apricot-buff blossoms.

Roses can be very utilitarian. Dense, thorny roses, when planted in masses along your property boundaries, make good barriers. A hedge of tall roses also makes a good visual screen that can be much prettier to look at than the neighbor's backyard. Low-growing Ground Cover roses are a beautiful alternative to lawn in sunny areas that you'd rather not mow, and the dense root system of many of these roses makes them ideal for securing slopes and preventing erosion. And roses placed throughout the landscape, especially along the woods' edge, around ponds, and beside streams, help create an ideal habitat for wildlife—providing food, shelter, and nesting sites.

Sometimes it's nice to devote an area of the landscape strictly to roses. The cutting garden, when it's a collection devoted solely to roses for cuttings rather than as a garden to be admired, is a practical planting best suited to areas beyond the immediate vicinity of the house. Rose bowers, particularly when benches have been placed beneath them, are appealing destinations in the landscape. And we can create informal garden areas—perhaps even secret, hidden gardens—filled with fragrant roses that are especially appealing to children that will give them a lifetime of memories and, perhaps, start them on their way to becoming lifelong gardeners.

As Alternative Ground Covers

While roses are traditionally used in beds bordered by lawns, they can also be used as an attractive alternative to lawns. I don't expect lawns to ever go out of style, simply because they are so useful—especially for young families with chil-

Choice Roses

for Landscape

'Bonica' 🌶 This was the first Modern Shrub rose to win the All-America Rose Selection Award (1987). Disease-resistant, 4- to 5-foot shrubs are literally smothered in pink blossoms in spring, with a scattering of flowers in summer and repeat bloom in autumn. Zone 4.

'Carefree Delight' 🌶 Resistant to mildew, black spot, and rose rust, this shrub reaches 4 to 5 feet, likes to sprawl, and should be allowed to do so. It makes a continuing display of pretty, single, carmine-pink flowers with cream-colored centers and yellow stamens. Zone 4.

'Henry Nevard' 🌶 A Hybrid Perpetual with large, fragrant, crimson roses on a 5-foot shrub. It has dark, leathery foliage that is resistant to black spot. Zone 5.

'Pink Meidiland' 🌶 This 4-foot shrub is a continuous bloomer with 2-inch, dark pink, single flowers. In the southeast, heat and humidity combine to encourage black spot;

'Sevillana'

otherwise, it's pest and disease resistant. Zone 4.

'Poulsen's Park Rose' 🌶 This large shrub has a vigorous, upright habit and lots of trusses of silver-pink flowers that repeat bloom later in the season. Zone 4.

'Roundelay' 🌶 A continuous-blooming, 4-foot shrub that produces lipstick-red, double, fragrant blossoms in large sprays. Zone 5.

'Sea Foam' 🌶 A large shrub that spreads to 6 feet across, with repeat-blooming clusters lightly fragrant, double roses of a pinkish-cream hue. Zone 5.

'Sevillana' 🌶 Also known as 'La Sevillana', this 4-foot shrub will spread to 5 feet across and produce semidouble clusters of bright red flowers all summer. Zone 6.

'The Fairy' 🌶 Although a Polyantha, 'The Fairy' is used as a Modern Landscape rose. It reaches just 2 feet, but spreads to 4 feet or more, making it an excellent edging, ground cover, and mixed-border plant. It continuously produces clusters of small, pink roses. Zone 5.

dren who need a place to run and play. However, lawns are very high-maintenance plantings that require constant care—weekly mowing, frequent fertilization, irrigation in hot, dry weather, and, all too often, heavy-duty weed and pest control. So why not replace at least some of your lawn with large masses of low-growing roses? Large masses of roses are especially suitable along a long, curving driveway; at the fringes of an orchard or vineyard; or anywhere that you have distant views. If you like, you can back these low-growing roses with masses of larger roses, shrubs, and trees, and then create a series of garden paths to wind through them.

Clean and classy—that's the landscape effect of an island bed devoted entirely to the pure white flowers of the Modern Shrub rose 'White Meidiland'.

Massed roses look best when they follow the natural contour of the land, creating gently curving, free-form beds rather than straight or geometrically shaped beds. Sweep them around part of a rock garden, plant them under a sunny stone outcrop, or tuck them around a beautiful tree or sculpture.

Plant masses of roses in staggered rows on centers that are just less than half the normal width of a mature plant. For instance, if a rose ultimately grows to 6 feet wide, plant it approximately 2½ feet from its neighbors in all directions. Within just a few years, the roses will spread to create a solid mass of stems that intertwine at their edges. When they bloom, they will create a solid mass of color. Just remember to leave a few paths or stepping-stones in the beds so you can get in there for routine rose care.

Choose Lax Roses with Good Foliage

Once-blooming Ground Cover roses are your best choice for low-maintenance, massed plantings. They make a striking sight when they bloom in spring, and have attractive foliage that will look good during the off-season. Although there are continuous-blooming Ground Cover roses available, they require regular deadheading to produce good bloom throughout the season—which is quite a chore when you have masses of roses.

What you really want are lax roses with good foliage. The low-growing *R. wichurana* hybrids and *R. rugosa* hybrids fill these requirements. One rose for a large area is our North American native prairie rose (*R. setigera*), which will make a 12-foot circle of foliage and flowers, and will mound to 4 feet in the center. It's a low-maintenance, bright pink, cold-hardy rose with good disease resistance, and a good choice for out-of-the-way parts of the landscape. For smaller areas, a spreading Shrub rose like the Polyantha 'The Fairy' is a good choice for its double-pink flowers and pretty foliage. As a massed ground cover closer to the house, a smaller cultivar like 'Gourmet Popcorn' might be better. It is a Miniature rose with white flowers and golden centers that grows into rounded shrubs from 18 to 24 inches tall.

Massed roses look best when they follow the natural contour of the land, creating gently curving, free-form beds rather than straight or geometrically shaped beds.

A Dark Background for Ground Covers

A bed of Ground Cover roses will show its color better if plants with dark leaves are planted behind it. If plants with leaf color similar to roses are used behind the bed, the effect will be to blur the edge of the bed and emphasize the foliage rather than the flower color. Dark green, shrubby conifers; dwarf, red-purple myrobalan plums (*Prunus cerasifera*); and dark-leaved cultivars of Japanese barberry (*Berberis thunbergii*), among many other dark-foliaged plants, will help strengthen the definition of the rose bed.

Securing Slopes

Roses that grab the soil and spill their canes and foliage down a slope will not only dress up the slope, but also anchor the soil so that hard rains won't wash it away. Slopes with large, protruding stones or boulders are even better. When the roses are spilling down erosion-prone banks between large stones, any water that runs there will be slowed down even more—tossed this way and that, and given time to percolate into the soil.

In fact, if you're constructing a berm (a mounded area or hillock) to give your property some vertical dimension, consider adding some large boulders, which should be buried by at least one third so they are secured and look more natural. Plant low-growing roses amid the stones, but not so densely that the rocks are completely covered by the foliage. The effect you're looking for is that of a rocky hillside with roses washing down around the stones and boulders, hiding the line where the stones emerge from the soil.

Rocks, mulch, and flowing water would be a lifeless setting without the Miniature 'Millie Walters' and her cheerful, pink-blend roses singing on the berm above. (American Rose Society garden, Shreveport, LA)

Select Roses with Strong Root Systems

Ground Cover roses like *R. wichurana* and its hybrids have strong root systems that help control erosion on banks and at places where water tends to run strongly during heavy rains. The matted rose roots hold the soil together, and the stems slow the water flow. The Poulsen company of Denmark has developed a remontant 18-inch, semidouble, white rose named 'Kent' that would admirably suit this purpose. It spreads to about 3 feet and produces large quantities of flowers.

Some prostrate Ground Cover roses toss out long canes that will grow to lie

A dense planting of Miniature 'Meillandina' almost completely covers this berm, spilling its roses onto the pebble walkway in a charming effect.

relatively close to the ground, making a good mat. But don't expect all of them to be truly prostrate. Most, in fact, grow from 1 to 4 feet tall. And be aware that most are once-blooming roses, although there are a few stand-out rebloomers. Mix them with other plants that will bloom earlier or later in the season if you must have flowers on your bank at all times.

Like other roses, most Ground Cover roses used on a slope need sun to bloom well. Although a surprising number of them will tolerate some shade, bloom will be reduced. For full shade, choose other low-growing

Roses that grab the soil and spill their canes and foliage down a slope will not only dress up the slope, but also anchor the soil so that hard rains won't wash it away.

or spreading plants such as bugleweed (*Ajuga reptans*), Japanese painted fern (*Athyrium nipponicum*), hellebores (*Helleborus* spp.), lilyturf (*Liriope muscari*), and the too-seldom-used Allegheny spurge (*Pachysandra procumbens*).

Slopes with Steps

On slopes where there are steps, keep roses well off the walkway so they don't create a hazard. In fact, it's often best to edge the steps with low-growing perennials or grassy-looking plants like Japanese forest grass (*Hakonechloa macra* 'Aureola'), black lilyturf (*Ophiopogon planiscapus* 'Nigrescens'), or blue fescue (*Festuca glauca*), and then to place Ground Cover roses behind or among them. Farther away, you can create a backdrop of taller Shrub roses, other flowering shrubs, and evergreen shrubs and trees.

Along Property Boundaries

Whether you live in a suburban neighborhood or on acreage in the country, roses are appropriate along the outskirts of your property. Here, they can screen unwanted views, create barriers, mark property boundaries, provide a backdrop for other plantings, and even establish a habitat for wildlife.

Large or distant areas of the landscape that don't get a lot of attention need roses that don't demand a lot of attention. So the Hybrid Teas, Floribundas, Grandifloras, and similar types probably aren't the best choice for these areas, since they require proper fertilization, plenty of moisture, and tidying up through the season. Hybrids of *R. rugosa*, *R. spinosissima*, and *R. wichurana* are much better suited to large, informal areas where they will perform beautifully if simply left alone.

As Barriers and Hedges

Large, thorny, old rose bushes planted in hedges were always valuable for keeping away marauders, whether human or animal, and had the bonus of beautiful flowers. While roses might at first seem like a flimsy security

Roses are useful along your property boundaries where they can screen unwanted views, create barriers, provide a backdrop for other plantings, and establish a habitat for wildlife.

barrier, large tangles of R. *multiflora* and other thorny roses are almost impossible to breach without special protection.

Perhaps the most useful and pretty variety with the cruelest thorns is R. *bracteata* 'Mermaid'. It's extremely vigorous, with trailing stems that can reach 20 feet or more, and is perfect as a barrier when trained along a fence of some sort. It tolerates partial shade, is disease resistant, and is hardy to Zone 6. 'Mermaid' bears recurrent, large, single, light yellow blossoms with golden stamens in the centers. Its devilish thorns make pruning a dicey business, so plant it at the edge of the property where it can grow at will with little or no attention. If growing it along a fence, space the plants 10 feet apart and allow the tips of the shoots to intertwine.

Screening Views

Densely planted roses also make good visual screens, and are usually much prettier to look at than the neighbor's backyard. You can plant some tall roses en masse, mix them with other tall shrubs and small trees, or grow Climbers and Ramblers up a trellis or fence.

You can also screen unsightly landscape features—perhaps an old barn or shed that still serves its purpose but just isn't all that attractive—by simply covering them with roses. When I lived in Pennsylvania, there was an abandoned, rusting hulk of a truck at the upper end of my orchard, so I planted a 'Climbing Cécile Brünner' at either end, which completely swamped it in small, pink blossoms—turning an eyesore into an attractive view.

When the great tree *fell and only the ugly stump was left, this property owner decided to cover it with glory, supplied by 'Sander's White Rambler', a* **R.** *wichurana hybrid.*
(Norman Beal garden, Raleigh, NC)

In Meadows

A popular way to treat land just beyond the lawns and gardens surrounding the house is to create a meadow—a natural-looking area consisting primarily of native grasses and wildflowers. Often, a meadow will have several islands of desirable woody plants or ornamental grasses in it—such as a hardy *Miscanthus*, a multitrunked American filbert (*Corylus americana*), or a modest-sized tree. Modern Shrub roses can be massed by the woody plants, and a low-maintenance Rambler like 'Seagull' or a large, open-branched, *R. spinosissima* hybrid like 'Frühlingsmorgen' can be grown into the limbs of trees.

At the transition from lawn to woods, where birds like to nest, 'Mary Rose', a pink Austin hybrid, joins the white Floribunda 'Iceberg' in beautifying the neighborhood. *(Patty and Jeff Daniels garden, Encinitas, CA)*

If there is a large boulder or several rocks in the meadow, that's the perfect place for a low-maintenance Rambler or Climber like 'Phyllis Bide' or 'Paul's Scarlet Climber' that can tumble up and over the rocks. Their June flowers will call attention to the meadow, and their fall hips will provide food for birds and animals through winter. Choose roses with softer, more natural colors—pale pinks and whites, especially. Bold colors—particularly the bright oranges and strong reds—look out of place in a naturalistic meadow and are best reserved for gardens near the house.

If you seed perennial wildflowers in the parts of the meadow, make sure that the plants are native to your region or that they thrive there. Many wildflower mixes contain seeds of plants that won't grow in your area, so read the label carefully and do a little research before purchasing. These areas of the meadow should be cut back with a sickle-bar mower in late fall or early spring to remove any woody saplings or tough briars that have grown up among the grasses and wildflowers.

Place your islands randomly, and give them graceful, curving edges rather that spotting them in polka-dot fashion. Paths may be as simple as mown strips through the meadow, or perhaps mulched paths edged in strips of wood or fallen tree limbs.

A Habitat at the Woods' Edge

Although most gardens are not designed with wildlife in mind, each provides something for the wildlife that visits it—chiefly food, shelter, and, in many cases, water. Roses play an especially important ecological role for birds. The dense, thorny thickets of rosebushes make fine shelter, protect birds from larger predators such as cats and squirrels when the nesting season begins, and attract plenty of food in the form of insects. And rose's colorful hips provide nutritious food for a multitude of wild creatures.

The woodland edge—where large trees give way to shrubs and then to forbs—is one of the most biologically rich parts of any property. Most birds and mammals, much like human beings, prefer to live in a protected area that looks out on a wide vista, and that's what the edge of the woods provides.

Choose low-maintenance, shade-tolerant Shrub roses to mix naturally with the native shrubs that colonize a woods' edge. The vigorous, apple-scented 'Lady Penzance'; the beautifully fragrant, white R. alba 'Semi-plena'; the double, white R. pimpinellifolia hybrid 'Karl Förster'; and the widely available, single, pink 'Complicata' are all perfectly suited for a woods' edge.

Many vigorous, shade-tolerant roses are also suited for climbing into trees along the woodland edge. The eglantine rose (R. eglanteria) likes to clamber up into shrubs and small trees, and one of its hybrids, 'Lady Penzance', which can be grown as a shrub or modest climber, has stunning cup-shaped, single, pink blossoms with lighter centers, and produces a reliable crop of hips for fall. The field rose (R. arvensis) is a vigorous,

Choose low-maintenance, shade-tolerant Shrub roses to mix naturally with the native shrubs that colonize a woods' edge.

Establishing Woods' Edge Climbers

Almost all roses like good soil, adequate water, and lots of light. The problem with the woods' edge is that the spot may be shady and the soil is often little more than an underground tangle of tree and shrub roots, which can greedily exhaust soil moisture and nutrients, leaving little for a young rose trying to become established. So find a spot among the trees and shrubs as open to sunlight as possible, but with the shrub or tree to be climbed still within reach of the rose canes.

Dig a generous hole for the rose, and chop away any roots in a 3-foot diameter. Plant the rose in native soil that has been mixed with a few handfuls of compost, and then cover the area with another 6 inches of compost. Water your rose until it has become established among the other plants.

shade-tolerant European native with single, white flowers. *R. arvensis* 'Splendens' has semidouble, white flowers and a pretty scent; both the species and cultivar will climb through tall shrubs and trees at the woods' edge. Of course, perhaps the best climber for this purpose is the Himalayan Musk rose (*R. filipes* 'Kiftsgate'). It is extremely vigorous and shade tolerant, and has the ability to scramble up your tallest tree, then come spilling out in an explosion of single, white flowers in early summer, which are later followed by a profusion of hips.

Reflecting at the Water's Edge

The effect of roses by water—reflecting in a glassy pool, cascading down from a constructed arch, tumbling out of waterside trees or shattering in a breeze and strewing petals on the water—is so superb that those with water features in their landscapes should surely consider their use. Those without a water feature might well make one just for the association with roses.

If the water is a natural lake, pond, slough, or stream, be aware that most roses don't like wet feet. (One exception is *R. californica*, but it's not especially suited for display around a landscaped water feature.) So if your water is bordered by marshy land, you'll need to plant roses far enough up a bank or away from the wetland so that there's good drainage. While improving basic soil structure is relatively easy, improv-

Rosa rugosa *is native to the northern seashore where wind and salt might be deadly to other varieties of roses. Here, they form the boundary between a lawn and the salt marsh beyond. (Alice Levien garden, Cutchogue, NY)*

ing drainage in an area is a big job. It can involve channeling water, installing French drains, and other significant and costly efforts. So my advice is to keep roses away from marshy land.

Oftentimes, however, a natural lake, pond, or stream will have banked sides with excellent drainage and a border of trees and shrubs. Here's your chance to grow some very floriferous Climbers, Ramblers, or

*Use bright colors—
especially strong pinks,
whites, and yellows—
that will stand out when
reflected off dark water.*

A comfortable, *quiet bower is formed using an arbor as structure. 'Iceberg' Floribundas flank the arbor, which is topped with* **Solanum jasminoides,** *known commonly, and inelegantly, as potato vine.* (Carol Brewer garden, El Cajon, CA)

species roses trained up into the trees so they can come tumbling out. Some of the smaller, pendulous roses such as 'Belle Amour', 'Cerise Bouquet', 'Alberic Barbier', 'Albertine', and 'Evangeline' will scale and twine through 6- to 10-foot shrubs of the wild types that border the water on one side and the woods behind them.

Man-made water features—created either by homeowners or hired landscape professionals—are wonderful additions to the residential landscape. Roses are lovely surrounding these small lily ponds, goldfish ponds, and the like. In these cozy surroundings, almost any moderately sized, upright Shrub or Landscape rose mingles beautifully with perennials to create a pond-side garden. And by all means, use bright colors—especially the strong pinks, whites, and yellows that will stand out when reflected off the dark water.

A Rose Bower, or Hideaway

Titania was neither the first nor the last female to awaken in her bower—her shaded, leafy, love nest—to find that her lover, of whom she was so enamored the previous night, was an ass. Be that as it may, a rose bower remains a superb and scented site for a romantic picnic or quiet getaway.

Although a bower could be formed beneath a man-made arch or arbor, one tends to think of it as a natural site—a small cove created by arching trees covered with leafy vines and roses. Rangy understory trees—which can be bent over and woven together at the tops to form a natural arch—are ideal for its structure. Among my favorite trees for creating bowers are the redbuds (*Cercis canadensis* and *C. occidentalis*), the golden chain tree (*Laburnum × watereri* 'Vossii'), semidwarf fruit trees like apples, pears, plums, and cherries planted close enough that their branches can be intertwined, and the common witch hazel (*Hamamelis virginiana*). For a backdrop, I like tall English yews (*Taxus baccata*), whose dark needles show off roses at their finest.

Choice Roses for Bowers

For candidate bower roses, two Climbers come immediately to mind. 'Climbing Cécile Brünner', the sweetheart rose, is a continual summer bloomer with fragrant, small, pink roses just right for this purpose. If things work out sweetheart-wise, you could add 'Wedding Day' on the other side of the bower. It produces huge trusses of single, fragrant roses that open a very soft yellow and fade to a whitish pink.

For sheer beauty in a shady spot, it's hard to beat the very vigorous 'Kew Rambler', with dense clusters of single, slightly cupped flowers of cotton-candy pink that fade to white centers where golden stamens cluster. If the spot is in full sun, 'Don Juan' might wander up one side of the bower, producing very double, extremely fragrant, dark red flowers that look like they should be pinned to the lapel of every Spanish Lothario, or held in the teeth of his lover.

If 'Don Juan' grows up one side, an appropriate 8- to 10-foot rambler for the other side would be the aptly named 'Alida Lovett'. She has fragrant,

A thornless rose, '*Mme. Legras de St. Germain' is a vigorous-growing Alba with strongly perfumed flowers that climbs to 7 feet or more.*

feminine, shell-pink flowers in clusters with petals that shade to gold toward their bases. If 'Don Juan' and 'Alida Lovett' really get along, perhaps they could use the services of 'Rambling Rector', a very vigorous rose that will take over the bower if allowed to ramble freely. It produces fragrant clusters of semidouble flowers followed by lots of pretty, light orange hips.

Thornless Roses a Plus in the Bower

For sheer romantic beauty, look for 'Ghislaine de Féligonde', a Multiflora Rambler that reaches to just 8 feet or so, with almost thornless stems—a nice feature in a rose bower where, if the bower floor is littered with thorny detritus, any impetus to romance could be painfully thwarted. Pale orange-yellow flowers with glowing, yellow centers are gorgeous in shape, and rebloom sparingly through the season. It tolerates some shade as well. Add a touch of romance with the modest, single, white-flowered, fragrant 'Silver Moon', and if, despite your labors, love is lost and romance turns frosty, look no further than 'Climbing Iceberg'.

Of course, if I were to be pinned down to only one rose for the bower, it would have to be 'New Dawn', probably the prettiest of the *R. wichurana* hybrids. This exquisite rose, of the softest blush pink, has semidouble blooms of perfect shape and lovely fragrance. It's a well-behaved Climber, with slender stems that reach 10 feet or so.

Companions for Bower Plantings

Other plants to grow over the bower along with your roses include any of the *Clematis* tribe. Few sights are as romantic and luscious as the pink, large-flowered *Clematis* 'Nelly Moser' joined by the dark red-violet and purple *Clematis* 'Dr. Ruppel'. One of my favorite plant combinations of all is the dark violet *Clematis* 'Niobe' grown with the rose 'New Dawn'.

The Virginia creeper (*Parthenocissus quinquefolia*), for its fall color, and American bittersweet (*Celastrus scandens*), for its showy fall berries, are two vigorous climbers that can help fill in the bower. In Zone 9 or 10,

If I were to be pinned down to only one rose for the bower, it would have to be 'New Dawn'.

The Modern Shrub rose 'Country Dancer' (foreground) sets the stage for the Modern Climbing rose 'Winghaven's White', which forms a thick and floriferous bower (background). (Pat and Stan Henry garden, Laurens, SC)

there's the Confederate vine (*Antigonon leptopus*), with chains of bright pink flowers that trail over heart-shaped leaves in the fall when roses rebloom. A hardier vine (to Zone 5) with salmon-red trumpets from July to September is trumpet vine (*Campsis* × *tagliabuana* 'Mme. Galen'). Continuing the theme, don't forget the hardier species of jasmines (*Jasminum* spp.), honeysuckles (*Lonicera* spp.), and passionflowers (*Passiflora* spp.).

A cutting garden *isn't usually designed— but it can't help being beautiful when planted with the white Floribunda 'Iceberg' (right) and the apricot-blend Austin rose 'Jaquenetta' (left).* (Pat and Stan Henry garden, Laurens, SC)

Although you have to live in Zone 9 to grow it outdoors, there is one vine perfectly suited to a romantic bower: the bower plant (*Pandorea jasminoides*). It's evergreen and grows to 20 feet, producing blushing pink trumpets, 2 inches wide at the mouths, in clusters of four to eight blossoms, from June to October. Prune it annually in spring to promote bushy growth, and grow it over the bower with a dark pink Climbing rose like 'Pink Perpetue'.

Carpet the Bower's Floor

The following plants can be useful as soft cushioning on the floor of the rose bower. Both woodland phlox (*Phlox divaricata*) and creeping phlox (*P. stolonifera*) are soft ground covers. Periwinkle (*Vinca minor*) can take a little crushing without much harm. In warm zones, baby's tears (*Soleirolia soleirolii*) makes a soft mat that is easily disturbed by crushing, but quickly repairs any damage because of its strong growth. Pearlwort (*Sagina subulata*) also takes some foot traffic. Sandwort (*Arenaria* spp.) is similar to pearlwort in appearance and function. Maiden pinks (*Dianthus deltoids* and *D.* 'Tiny Rubies') make low mats of grass-like foliage, with pretty flowers on short stalks. Lilyturf (*Liriope muscari*), black lilyturf (*Ophiopogon planiscapus* 'Nigrescens'), and Allegheny spurge (*Pachysandra procumbens*) all make excellent ground covers under a rose bower. All the above will thrive in filtered light. The edges of the bower can be planted with the easy-care native narrow-leaved spleenwort (*Athyrium pycnocarpon*).

Should you make a rose bower and decide to have a romantic picnic there, consider serving a well-chilled rose wine and perhaps the quail in rose petal sauce that you may remember from Laura Esquivel's *Like Water for Chocolate*. In the book and the movie, Tita makes this dish from roses given to her by her secret lover, Pedro. After eating it, Tita's sister Gertrudis is so enflamed, she literally sets the shower stall on fire. At that point, one of Pancho Villa's troops appears on horseback, swings the naked Gertrudis up to his saddle, and gallops away with her. The recipe is in Esquivel's book, if you dare.

> *Baby's tears makes a soft mat beneath a bower that is easily disturbed by crushing, but quickly repairs any damage because of its strong growth.*

The Ultimate Rose Bower Companion

If you live in California or the warm areas of the Sun Belt, you can grow star jasmine (*Trachelospermum jasminoides*), the perfect companion for roses in a bower. Here's a plant of incredible diversity: Most important, its small white flowers project its sweet, heady scent across dozens of feet in June and July; it grows equally well in shade or sun; it will make a ground-covering mat or grow up bower supports; it likes water but will do fine during droughts. And it has no thorns.

Choice Roses

for Large, Informal Landscapes

'Alida Lovett'  This *R. wichurana* hybrid has double, old-fashioned, mildly scented blooms of soft, shell pink changing to yellow near the petal bases. It blooms in June. Zone 5.

'Blanc Double de Coubert' This *R. rugosa* hybrid has pure-white, double flowers with a rich scent. It is a repeat bloomer, and has lots of hips and golden fall color. Zone 3.

'Delicata' Another repeat-blooming *R. rugosa* hybrid with beautiful, crinkly foliage and clusters of semi-double, rosy-pink flowers followed by sizeable hips. Zone 4.

'Frühlingsgold' The semidouble flowers of this *R. spinosissima* hybrid are gold fading to a soft, pastel yellow. It flowers in spring, makes a 6-foot shrub, and is nearly maintenance-free. Zone 4.

'Hansa' One of the best of the *R. rugosa* tribe, with large, fragrant, double, red-violet flowers continuously through the season, large hips, and lovely dark foliage. Zone 4.

'New Dawn' Beautiful pale pink, high-budded, double roses unfurl to perfume the air. This *R. wichurana* hybrid can climb or sprawl over difficult terrain. Unlike most of this group, it blooms well from June to frost. Zone 5.

R. setigera The native American prairie rose grows 4 feet tall and 12 feet across, blooms in midsummer with bright pink, fragrant, single flowers, and is hardy and disease resistant. Zone 3.

'Sanders' White Rambler' Pure-white, double flowers appear in both large and small clusters over this sprawling rose. A vigorous *R. wichurana* hybrid that blooms once in late June and can be trained like a climber. Zone 5.

'Scabrosa' Silvery cherry-mauve, single flowers with prominent golden stamens bloom continuously on 6-foot plants, freely producing large hips. This *R. rugosa* hybrid is fragrant and makes a dense, 6-foot shrub. Zone 4.

'Stanwell Perpetual' A very hardy rose with pale pink, double, old-fashioned flowers that repeat bloom through the season. A *R. spinosisima* hybrid, it grows to 5 feet tall and displays attractive foliage. Zone 3.

'Stanwell Perpetual'

Cutting Gardens

As roses take over more of your life, you may find yourself building a special collection of plants. You may be taking cuttings from them to propagate new roses, or perhaps you want lots of fresh roses in arrangements with other flowers and foliage for your house, or you use them for making potpourri, rose water, candied rose petals, and such. For these purposes, it's nice to have a special garden reserved just for these hard-working roses so that you can take all the cuttings you want without your garden looking plundered.

Such practical rose beds are usually located out of view—away from the house, but not so far away that you won't visit them regularly. Even those who live on a small lot can find a spot behind a garage, on a less-traveled side of the house, or behind a hedge of shrubbery.

Since these are working gardens, easily accessible rows of roses with paths on either side make the most sense. If possible, make your paths 3 to 4 feet wide. This provides plenty of room for working, and will be wide enough for a garden cart. Plant your roses single file down the rows so that you can easily reach them from both sides. If your roses reach 3 to 4 feet in diameter when fully grown, you can place four roses down a 15-foot row. Mulch under the roses to keep weeds down and improve the soil, and keep the paths mown closely or covered in mulch. Plantings of low-growing perennials such as *Aubrieta*, *Alyssum*, or other mounding perennials can be placed here and there to dress up the scene, but that's not really necessary, given the nature of the planting.

Roses for cutting line this nicely mulched pathway. At the far turn, the small, pink roses are the Polyantha 'China Doll', while between them is the larger Floribunda 'Else Poulsen'. *(Pat and Stan Henry garden, Laurens, SC)*

Mulch under the roses in your cutting garden to keep weeds down and improve the soil.

Gardens for Children

Over my 30-plus years as a garden writer and television host interviewing gardeners about their gardens, I've often asked folks what inspired them to create their beautiful landscapes, especially their choice of roses. The most frequent answer is, "I remember how my grandmother's (or, often, mother's) garden looked. I want mine to look like that."

It's true with me, too. My mother loved roses, and the rear patio behind our country house in the Pocono Mountains of Pennsylvania was decorated with roses on the walls, roses on trellises, and roses along the fences that formed the patio's boundaries. It was there, in our rose gardens, that I learned how to use a weeder, and learned not to kneel on the

__Any garden__ meant to please and intrigue children will have plenty of birdhouses. This fine apartment is flanked by the Modern Shrub rose 'Sea Foam'.

old rose-cane trimmings unless I wanted a thorn in my knee. I came to love roses anyway.

As you go about designing your landscape with roses, be aware that when youngsters come to visit, especially kids from ages four through seven, they are storing up memories, like seeds that may one day sprout and grow and bloom to make the next generation of rose gardens and landscapes. You and I are links in a long chain of rose lovers that extends back to the time when hunter-gatherers must have marked the place where the pretty, scented flowers grew and returned in the fall to gather the nutritious, vitamin C-rich hips.

A Child's Rose Garden

To create a rose garden for children, think about what delights children most. Bright colors, for sure. Big, blowsy double roses with petals for scattering. Bright red hips for nibbling and tasting a tiny sour kiss. And perfumy fragrance, too. Here are some ideas:

- Place a swing, fishpond, or playhouse at the end of a rose-bordered path.
- Go on a safari with your children. See how many insects, spiders, worms, and other wildlife you can find in the rose garden.
- Roll some rose beads from cooked petals of fragrant roses and string them to dry, or freeze petals in ice cubes for adding to sodas and iced tea.
- Plant strawberries, currants, blueberries, dwarf fruit trees, and bramble fruits among your roses. Go hunting and gathering with the kids, and bring home some pretty flowers with the berries.
- Don't forget to include a sundial, birdbath, bird feeder, or small statues of creatures like frogs and foxes among your roses to delight the children.

A Bouquet of Roses

The density and sheltering ability of roses and the addition of some garden furniture can easily create bowers and hideaways for you, the kids, or anyone who needs to find a quiet moment among the roses. The idea of a children's garden featuring roses is a good theme for the landscape. Here's a place for children to be exposed to not only bright color and fragrance, but also the pollinators who visit the roses, and the thorns that life has prepared for the unwary.

While children may not like thorns, that doesn't mean they can't live with a few thorny specimens in their garden, especially if they're grown for cutting so that children can make their own bouquets for the house. I do believe we tend to micromanage children, and so I recommend giving children a bucket of water and setting them loose in the cutting garden to create an arrangement of roses that they think will be beautiful. Just give them some simple tips on how to take cuttings properly; you'll be surprised at just how well they do.

While children may not like thorns, that doesn't mean they can't live with a few thorny specimens in their garden.

Children *will first run to play on the rope ladder, but then discover the sweet scent of the Modern Climbing rose 'City of York', and, later in the year, the apples that will ripen in the tree.* (Anne McIntyre garden, Chipping Norton, Oxfordshire, England)

Miniature Roses with Playful Names

Miniature roses are perfect for the children's garden for a couple of reasons. First and foremost, they are relatively foolproof—disease resistant, hardy, and very floriferous—so children don't have to watch dismayed as their rose succumbs to rust or black spot. Second, their small size may intrigue the child, although in my experience with kids, it's often "the bigger the better." Anything odd-sized, whether very large or very small, seems to perk up their imaginations. If you incorporate some miniatures, plant them in terra-cotta pots or edge a border with them.

Choose varieties with childlike names, such as 'Teddy Bear', 'Cinderella', 'Baby Darling', 'Hula Girl', 'Lollipop', 'Party Girl', 'Plum Pudding', 'Rose Baby', 'Snookie', 'Sweet Fairy', 'Toy Clown', or 'Yellow Doll'. What child won't want to take a trip to the garden to see how 'Snookie' is doing?

Finally, don't forget the accoutrements that make a garden special for a child. Invite wildlife in with a shallow pond, a birdbath, or bird feeder, and berried plants that birds love, like mulberries and autumn olive. Other features that kids enjoy include a sundial, a swing (especially those Victorian glider swings in a frame), and statuary like a small stone fox or frog peeking out of the ferns. Add a whirligig—one of those contraptions that operates when the wind blows. They're usually made in someone's garage and often sold at flea markets. Kids (of all ages) love them.

A garden of bright color, beautiful fragrance, and lots of goodies to discover and eat—as well as a place to hide under the cover of a blooming rose—is a child's paradise and a paradise for anyone still young at heart.

One way *to teach a child the name of a rose would be to set a bowl of popcorn on this kid-sized table and inform the child that the little rose behind her is a Miniature named 'Popcorn'.* (Susan Price garden, Petaluma, CA)

Two kinds of fencing—
white pickets and rustic sapling poles—support the apricot-pink English rose 'Ellen'; the single, silvery-pink Hybrid Tea 'Dainty Bess'; and the tall Floribunda 'Poulsen's Pearl'. (Anna Davis garden, Atlanta, GA)

Chapter 6

On Structures

O NE OF THE MOST DELIGHTFUL ways to use roses in the landscape is to grow them on decorative yet functional structures— trellises, arbors, arches, pillars, pergolas, gazebos, and fences. In the late Victorian period, such structures were at the height of their popularity, and homeowners bedecked their landscapes with them. But by the latter half of the 20th century, the more elaborate and decorative structures had quietly disappeared from the landscape. More recently, along with the renewed interest in Old Garden roses, these decorative structures have once again found a home in American gardens.

167

A simple fence *gives a vertical dimension to the garden, allowing for displays like deep-red 'Don Juan', a fragrant Modern Climbing rose, joined by the cool colors of sweet peas and foxgloves.* (Sutter Home Vineyard garden, St. Helena, CA)

New building materials and tools, along with prefabrication techniques, have made them more affordable and available to all homeowners.

As a general rule, arches, trellises, and pillars are the simplest of structures; arbors and pergolas can be either casual or grand; and gazebos, no matter what their style, tend to be the grandest of all garden structures. A pergola will make the strongest visual impact of just about any garden structure, especially when it's clothed in blooming roses. Arches and trellises take the least space, arbors and gazebos more space, and pergolas the most space of all. However, with some careful planning, even a small yard can support any of them, except, perhaps, for a gazebo, which needs a good swath of lawn around it to give it a setting. Fences have been, and will always be, an essential landscaping element—so why not cloak them in a blanket of colorful blossoms?

Structures—whether built from painted wood, wrought iron, rough-hewn cedar, rhododendron, aged-copper pipes, or even heavy-duty molded plastic—add a much desired vertical element to the landscape, bringing the color and fragrance of roses and other vines to eye level and beyond. They're a wonderful way to display roses beyond beds and borders, and—at least with arches, arbors, pergolas, and gazebos—to lure strollers into new areas of the garden.

Choice Roses

among Repeat-Blooming Climbers

'America' ✿ This Climber has a rich perfume. It's a fully double Modern Climber with a continuous-blooming habit, salmon-red flowers, and canes that reach 25 feet. Zone 7.

'Climbing Iceberg' ✿ A vigorous, disease-resistant Climber that produces lots of semidouble, pure white flowers. It is a reliable continuous bloomer. Zone 5.

'Cramoisi Supérieur' ✿ The ball-shaped, double flowers of this China rose are a strikingly rich crimson, and the tips of its thin canes will droop prettily from a trellis if left unsupported. It has a long summer season. Zone 5.

'Dortmund' ✿ This is an introduction from Kordes, the renowned German hybridist. Its big, single blossoms are a rich crimson with a pale center. Canes reach to 10 feet. If deadheaded, it will repeat bloom. Zone 5.

'Honorine de Brabant' ✿ An old-fashioned Bourbon, this rose will climb modestly on a 6-foot trellis. Its lavender and purple blooms are very fragrant, and it flowers continuously all summer. Zone 5.

'Dortmund'

'New Dawn' ✿ An exceptional continuous-blooming rose with a vigorous growth habit. Semidouble, high-centered buds open to fragrant roses of the most luscious shell pink. One of the most beautiful varieties for trellising. Zone 5.

'Parade' ✿ An offspring of 'New Dawn', it is disease resistant, blooms continuously, and has a sweet fragrance. Its double roses are a rich pink that will be a standout when planted with red roses or blue morning glories. Canes reach about 10 feet. Zone 5.

'Sombreuil' ✿ This rose climbs only to about 8 feet, but is still worth training on a trellis. Its very double, flat roses of creamy to pure white carry a delicious scent. This old-fashioned, repeat-blooming Climbing Tea has been cherished since the mid-19th century. Zone 7.

'White Cockade' ✿ Another offspring of 'New Dawn', but of a clean, white color with a double, Tea form and sweet, delicate scent. Its canes grow to 8 feet and produce flowers all summer. Zone 5.

'America'

If large enough and freestanding, a trellis can function as a wall or divider to create distinct garden rooms.

Splayed against Trellises

A trellis is an upright panel, fan, or other structure that can be freestanding, attached to a house or other building, or even placed in a container. It is often, but not always, made from lattice or other crisscrossing materials. If large enough and freestanding, it can function as a wall or divider to create distinct, separate garden rooms. Vase-shaped trellising, readily available at garden and home centers, is an excellent choice as it naturally leads rose canes up and out at an angle that helps them intercept more sunlight. This kind of outward-splaying trellis fits nicely into planting boxes, and the less vigorous types of climbers or even taller shrub roses can be trained to them and set on decks, patios, and porches.

Controlling Views

A trellis is frequently used to screen areas from view, but just as often *is* the view—an attractive focal point draped in roses and other vines. Think of the tall, arching, pure pink 'Constance Spry' intertwined with the contrasting but harmonious, rich burgundy and purple *Clematis* 'Dr. Ruppel'. Picture it commingled with a variegated kiwi vine (*Actinidia kolomikta*), whose pink-edged leaves match the pink of the rose. Or imagine an annual morning glory like *Ipomoea tricolor* 'Heavenly Blue' blazing away among the salmon-pink blooms of climbing 'Galway Bay' or rich red roses of 'Dublin Bay'. A trellis can also serve as an attractive backdrop to other plantings—perhaps a mixed bed of flowering shrubs, ornamental grasses, and colorful perennials.

Because of its attention-grabbing qualities, place trellising strategically throughout the landscape. For instance, if you have a straight path, place

The strong perspective of the trellis leads the eye to the sunburst design of the bench. The gardener has wisely planted the continuous-blooming R. wichurana hybrid 'New Dawn' at just the right spot to soften the hard lines and emphasize the focal point. (Michael Shoup garden, Brenham, TX)

a trellis at the end of that path as a focal point. It will give your eyes a visual stopping point, and even redirect them back into the garden. A statue, pedestal, fountain, or some other interesting object placed in front of the trellis is a nice added touch that can add the element of surprise.

Screening Unwanted Views

Building or placing a trellis is one of the easiest ways to screen an area or hide an eyesore—perhaps a metal garden shed, propane tank, swimming pool pumps, air-conditioning unit, or the neighbor's trash cans. You can do this one of two ways: First, enclose the object on all four sides, covering three with roses and leaving the fourth hinged and unplanted for access. Second, simply place the trellis between your viewing position and the object to be screened.

For year-round screening and good looks, mix other vines with roses, especially dense vines with lots of foliage. In winter, evergreen foliage

When you want to screen a view, a trellis provides the scaffolding and roses do the job. The red Hybrid Kordesii 'Illusion' and light lavender-pink Hybrid Musk 'Lavender Lassie' are dense, short Climbers that bloom on and on all summer long. (New York Botanical Garden, Bronx, NY)

Placed at the end of a path, a trellis will give your eyes a visual stopping point and even redirect them back into the garden.

**'Eden', a Modern Climbing rose, tosses
its sprays of cream and lavender-pink roses
through the cross members of a simple
trellis.**

will be especially helpful in providing a continuous screen. But even without foliage, a dense tangle of roses and vines on trellising will continue to hide what's behind them. Many people use honeysuckle for this purpose, but don't plant the rampant, sometimes invasive Japanese honeysuckle (*Lonicera japonica* 'Halliana'). There are better-behaved choices among the honeysuckles, including woodbine (*L. periclymenum*), the semievergreen honeysuckle (*L. heckrottii*), yellow honeysuckle (*L. flava*), and the biggest of all, perfect for joining roses in covering structures, the trumpet honeysuckle (*L. sempervirens*).

Creating Privacy

Trellises can also be used as screens to create privacy, especially in small, suburban backyards where you need to use all the space you have. A freestanding, rose-covered trellis takes up much less space than a hedge or grouping of evergreen trees, but can provide just as much privacy. It would certainly be more colorful than evergreens, and would require less upkeep than many hedges.

An alternative to a freestanding trellis is a solid, 4-foot fence topped with a 3-foot section of trellis. This provides more privacy but offers less trellising for roses to hang on to. Another option is to mix or alternate trellises or trellis-topped fences with open spaces, low fences, or low hedges. This is a good way to preserve desirable vistas while screening out unwanted views, and it makes a small yard feel a little less hemmed in.

The Problem with Wall Trellising

While prefabricated wooden lattice or trellising can be fixed to walls where it can serve as scaffolding for climbing roses, it's not a good idea to use it this way unless you can keep the vegetation on the outside of the trellis. The problem is that canes will grow through the trellising or latticework and become crowded and mildew prone back there. Not only that, but pruning becomes a bear of a chore when canes are behind latticework, and may, in some cases, require dismantling the whole

Building a Trellis-Topped Fence

Afreestanding trellis needs a sturdy base, as the weight of roses on a flimsy trellis will soon pull it over, if not down. One way to solve the problem is to build a fence with 4 feet of solid boards topped by 3 feet of lattice that will support climbing roses. You can a build single section for screening, or multiple sections as a solid fence around your yard or a swimming pool.

Start by sinking sturdy, 8½-foot, 4x4 posts of cedar, black locust, redwood, or pressure-treated lumber and placed at 8-foot intervals, at least 18 inches into cement in the ground so that their tops are 7 feet above ground level. Strong horizontal supports—two rows of 2x4s, with one row about 1 foot off the ground and the other at 4 feet—are added to hold vertical fencing boards. Cut these supports to size (approximately 7 feet 8 inches, but measure the distance between your posts to be exact), and mount them with L-brackets to the posts; the supports should be flush with the side on which you'll mount the fencing. Next, tack on 1x6 fencing boards cut 3 feet 8 inches long, leaving about 4 inches between the bottom of the board and the ground and about a nail's width between the boards.

Above the fencing, you'll add 3-foot sections of lattice, which is a standard width available at most lumberyards. Cut them to length (approximately 8 feet, but measure carefully so that they can be mounted directly on the posts), attach some 1-inch lathing strips around the edge for trim, and nail the lattice to the posts. For added protection, coat the whole fence, including the trellis top, with a sealer. If you like, you can use one that also includes stain.

And finally, finish your trellis-topped fence by planting roses at intervals appropriate to their size. Climbers that reach 10 to 12 feet would probably look best planted at 8-foot intervals. I prefer planting the roses on the back side of the fence, so that what you see are roses twining through the trellising and tumbling a bit down the front. The back of the fence still looks nice, as there are roses planted and flowering there. Just make sure your roses will receive enough light on the side that you plant them.

Top a solid fence with sections of lattice, and train roses along them.

When roses are planted on the shady side of a trellis, they tend to grow through it to find more sun, as the Hybrid Tea 'Eden' is doing here. This allows more of the structure to be seen—an advantage with a pretty trellis like this one.

Color for the Trellis

While natural wood trellising looks perfectly fine, you can also color your trellis and coordinate its color with a rose. Before installing the trellis, spray-paint it with outdoor enamel; a matte finish looks best. Try red or yellow roses on a blue trellis, or orange roses on a burgundy or red-brown trellis. As a general rule, avoid "hard" or brilliant paint colors; use pastels or natural-looking colors instead.

structure just to prune properly (which neither you, nor I, nor any sane person would do, and so the problem would be left unattended).

However, if you're willing to make sure that the roses are kept from growing behind the trellising, or the trellis is far enough away from the wall that you can get back in there to prune, you will get a fine visual result.

Positioning for Sunlight

A trellis can be positioned to face in any direction (and, in fact, a freestanding trellis faces two directions), but growing roses on a south-facing trellis (or the south side of a trellis) makes the most sense, as this is where they will receive the most sun and produce the most flowers. West facing is the next most advantageous position, as the roses will intercept a lot of sunlight during the hot afternoon hours. Roses that tolerate a bit of shade will find a good home on an east-facing trellis where they receive morning sun and afternoon shade.

A north-facing location, however, will require Climbing roses that can really take some shade. And even these roses, although they may produce blooms, will not be as floriferous as roses grown in a sunnier location. You would think that you could grow a shade-tolerant rose on the north side of a trellis, and a sun-loving rose on the opposite, south side. I tried that once and found that while a rose may be shade tolerant, that doesn't mean it wouldn't like more sun. And so, it grows through the trellising and soon you have two roses on the south side and just a few sparse stems on the north side. So use one side of the trellis only, and make sure it is backed by a wall or trees that throw shade from the south.

It's well known that 'Gruss an Aachen' and 'Zéphirine Drouhin' are shade tolerant. Many other roses said to be shade tolerant, however, aren't actually well suited for shade. The reliably shade-tolerant varieties tend to be hybrids of *R. multiflora*, including many Hybrid Musks and Polyanthas. The Noisettes also are generally tolerant of some shade. Most shade-tolerant roses are pale in color, cluster flowered, fragrant, and disease resistant, and thrive in adverse conditions. They perform beautifully in sun, but their hardy constitution allows them to flower well in shade, too.

Notice how the roses *planted on the sunny side of the trellis obscure its structure, while the same rose—hybrid Kordesii 'Morgengrüss', tied up as a climber on the shady side—peeks through the trellis, giving a nice balance of plant and structure.*

When growing Climbing roses on a trellis, you'll get better bloom if you train the canes into somewhat horizontal positions.

'Wind Chimes', *a Hybrid Musk noted for its strong scent, has been planted alongside a walkway where its rich, sweet fragrance can easily be enjoyed by passersby.*

Attaching Climbers

When growing Climbing roses on a trellis, you'll get better bloom if you train the canes into somewhat horizontal positions. Bring a cane up for the first few feet, and then train it diagonally or sideways so that the cane receives as much sunlight along its length as possible. The sunlight will stimulate bloom in continuous-blooming varieties and ensure an abundance of flower buds for the following year on the once-blooming kinds.

Climbing roses aren't natural climbers—at least, not like grapevines with their tendrils, ivies with their aerial rootlets, morning glories with their twining habit, or clematis with their twisting leaf stems. They need to be supported and loosely tied in place. Use something soft and pliable, such as the green, plastic ribbon available at garden centers, to tie your rose canes to a trellis. Pieces of dark-colored cloth will also work. Avoid twist-ties, those paper-covered wires used to seal bread bags; the paper will disintegrate over time and the wires can cut into and injure expanding canes. Instead of just roping the stems to the trellis and tying them off with a square knot, use a figure-eight tie: Loop the ribbon around the cane; cross the ends; loop them around the trellis; then tie them together. Tie loosely rather than tightly, as young rose canes will need room to expand. The figure-eight loop will help keep bark from rubbing off the stems on a windy day.

Up and Over Arches

An arch is something you can walk through—like the extension above a gate. It can be curved, flat, or angular; freestanding or attached to another structure; a single arch or a series of arches. It most often marks the entrance to a new section in a garden, but a series of arches can span a pathway connecting two areas.

The delightful moon gate and extensive trellising—all painted a soft green that blends in with the small, single, red-and-white Hybrid Musk 'Mozart' and the tall Bourbon 'Mme. Isaac Pereire'—create the walls of an outdoor garden room.
(Anna Davis garden, Atlanta, GA)

Many manufacturers sell prefabricated wooden kits that come together easily into attractive arches that can be painted or left natural. I've placed one of these arches at the entryway to my pool and deck; it frames a gate in the deck's railing and supports a *Clematis montana* var. *rubens*. A simple, arched tunnel can be made from bent, metal rods or plastic tubing; simply slide them into slightly larger, hollow, metal pipes that have been driven into the ground on either side of your path. And then, if you like, connect the arches by tying them at their apexes to a pole that runs the length of the archway.

Planting an Arch

R. wichurana hybrids are good choices for arches. They are vigorous, multibranched roses that usually reach 15 feet—growing up and over the top, and partway down the other side of an arch. Rather than planting the same rose on the opposite side of the arch, opt for a Floribunda or other favorite Shrub rose that will reach up and touch the *R. wichurana* hybrid. If you have a series of arches, alternate the planting scheme at each arch—swapping the color-coordinated *R. wichurana* hybrid and Shrub rose to opposite sides—for a wonderful effect.

You can also plant Ramblers that will reach from one side of an arch all the way over to the ground on the other side. But remember that ramblers may be so vigorous that they simply overwhelm your archway. Choose them carefully or go with modest Climbers, one on either side, to meet at the apex.

Two posts *have been erected on a pathway through the garden. A Modern Climbing rose 'Rhonda' has been planted by each, with its long canes curved up and over, then tied together to form an archway. It's simple, easy, and effective.* (Pat and Stan Henry garden, Laurens, SC)

Choice Roses

for the Arbor

'Altissimo' ✿ This Modern Climbing rose sends up 10-foot canes with dark foliage and single, dark, cardinal-red flowers centered with puffs of yellow stamens. A good rose to combine with another Climber. Zone 5.

'Climbing Devoniensis' ✿ An old-fashioned, repeat-blooming Tea rose with large, creamy white, double flowers blushed with pink on 12-foot canes. The flowers have weak stems, so they nod downward from the top of the arbor. Zone 8.

'Climbing Iceberg' ✿ One of the few climbing sports of the Floribunda class, with all the shrub form's advantages plus the ability to reach 10 to 12 feet. Pure ivory flowers of beautiful form are produced continually, and grace its disease-resistant foliage. Zone 5.

'Golden Showers' ✿ A Modern Climbing rose that blooms continuously from June to October. The butter-yellow buds are pointed and open to fragrant, ruffled, pure yellow blossoms that fade to cream. It tolerates shade well. Zone 5.

'Kiftsgate' ✿ This rose flowers but once, yet the blossoms come late and stay through July. They appear in massive groups of hundreds of small, creamy-white cups holding puffs of yellow stamens. It will easily smother an arbor and might best be reserved for a pergola. Zone 7.

'Mme. Alfred Carrière' ✿ Continuous blooming and strongly fragrant, with large, white flowers tinged in pink, this climbing Noisette has a rather stiff, up-right habit that can be softened by tying it to the trellis. Zone 6.

'Mme. Grégoire Staechelin' ✿ A beautiful pale pink Hybrid Tea with superb fragrance. If deadheaded, it will produce several flushes of flowers on 15-foot canes. Zone 5.

'New Dawn' ✿ Modern Climbing rose produces pearly pink, sweet-smelling roses of the utmost sophistication and beauty, their large clusters recurring during the season. The canes reach 10 to 12 feet. Its plentiful foliage is usually disease free. A highly recommended rose for the arbor. Zone 5.

'Parade' ✿ The fragrance of this Modern Climbing rose is lovely, and the cherry-pink roses are fully double. A modest but vigorous grower, it reaches only 8 feet. Zone 5.

'Mme. Grégoire Staechelin'

'Sympathie' ✿ A Modern Climbing rose from Kordes, it grows to 12 feet with fragrant, high-centered, blood-red blossoms that bloom all summer. Zone 5.

'Veilchenblau' ✿ This almost thornless, 15-foot rose has big clusters of violet-purple flowers with white centers and clutches of yellow stamens that fade to lilac. It enjoys some shade. Zone 5.

The R. wichurana *hybrid* 'New Dawn'
festoons a beautiful arbor that leads
from one part of the garden to another.
(Kathy Whiteside garden, Madison, GA)

An arbor should be at least
5 feet wide and 7 feet
tall—big enough for
one person to walk
underneath comfortably.

Draping Arbors

An arbor is an open, framed, boxlike structure—either freestanding with four posts or pillars, or attached to a house or outbuilding with just two supporting posts or pillars. It makes a fine roof for a shady outdoor room, especially when timbers across its top support roses, grapevines, wisteria, or other vines. Place a picnic table or grouping of chairs beneath the arbor to create a shady sitting or dining area.

Sometimes arbors are little more than big arches—with four posts instead of two, and perhaps a series of crossbars or lattice covering them. Arbors can high-light the entrance to a house, patio, or pool house, or mark the transition from one garden area to another. They are the doorways through which we enter these places, and they are never more beautiful than when adorned with roses. Growing roses on an arbor attached to a doorway is a simple alternative to training roses up a wall and over a doorway in es-palier fashion.

Arbors Should Be Stout

Many building-supply centers, home and garden centers, and mail-order companies carry prefabricated arbors that are easily assembled. And con-structing an arbor from scratch doesn't have to be a complicated building project—although you can certainly make it so by erecting brick or mortared piers and columns, fancy-cut finials, and such. Just make sure your arbor is built of stout, sturdy materials and the posts are sunk into concrete or strapped with metal braces to concrete piers. Posts sunk into moist soil will rot out in short order.

An arbor should be at least 5 feet wide and 7 feet tall. This is big enough for one person to walk underneath comfortably, with plenty of room to spare, and it keeps the vegetation from grabbing the hats off the heads of passersby. It can be as deep as you want—12 feet or more to cover a patio for dining and relaxing, or just a couple of feet if it covers a gateway into an adjoining part of the garden or frames a doorway.

'Sally Holmes', a vigorous Hybrid Musk, not only beautifies the arbor that forms a delightful patio seating area, but also shades the patio below. (Helen and Arthur Dawson garden, La Jolla, CA)

An attached arbor opens new possibilities. *This one supports* Clematis 'Jackmanii' (left). *The Hybrid Musk 'Sally Holmes' reaches up to touch the out-of-bloom* Wisteria. *(Joy and George Wolff garden, Healdsburg, CA; designed by Greg Lowery)*

When attaching an arbor to a house, you can either leave the sides open or affix lattice to them, but it's a good idea to use 2x4s or sturdy poles across the top, as $\frac{1}{2}$-inch lattice up there will soon rot out under dense foliage or break under the weight of heavy vines. These arbors should be securely attached to the house or outbuilding with joist hangers.

Because an arbor adjacent to a house is so frequently seen, the roses there need more tending to keep looking their best. Too often the sides of rose arbors are simply a number of almost leafless, twisting, wickedly thorny canes that signal more of a warning than an invitation. Most of the foliage and almost all of the flowers are perched on top of the arbor, where they can hardly be seen, except from a second-story window. The canes at the top get the most sunlight, so they will be the more floriferous ones—smiling back up at the sun that called them forth, but leaving the gardener and her visitors out of sight down below.

Helping Rose Canes to Arch Downward

When young canes shoot out near the top of the arbor, keep them from growing straight up by placing spring-operated clothespins near their tips. Most clothespins have a slot for the clothesline that works just as well to hold the cane tip without crushing it. Use as many clothespins as it takes to get the cane arching downward. Once the cane wood hardens, it should stay in that position. The downward-arching cane has two advantages: one is visual appeal—a gracefully arching cane looks better than a stiffly upright one—and, second, it is a better position for receiving sunlight, which will result in more flower buds.

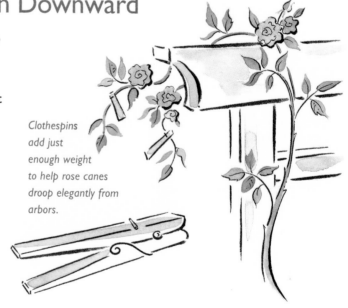

Clothespins add just enough weight to help rose canes droop elegantly from arbors.

What we want are roses in leaf and flower blooming up the sides of the arbor and along the top. You can manage this, but careful choice of cultivar is important here. To choose carefully, you need to know the different forms and habits of Climbers and Ramblers so you can put them to use to get the effect you want.

Distinguishing Climbers and Ramblers

Climbers tend to be rebloomers, which is all to the good, but they also tend to have stout, vigorous canes that, when they reach the top of the arbor, want to keep growing straight up; *you* want them to lean over and crawl along the top. If you bend them over and tie them along the horizontal supports atop the arbor, they tend to throw up strong vertical laterals that will be very floriferous the next season.

You can stimulate leaf and bloom up the sides by staggering the height of young canes when doing your late-winter or early-spring pruning. To do this, cut weak, one-year canes back to 18 to 24 inches; a slightly stronger one-year cane to about 3 feet; and a more vigorous one or two-year cane to 4 feet. Allow vigorous, older canes to reach the top and form the horizontal stems. All the canes will put out new growth that will flower the following season.

Unlike Climbers, Ramblers have slender, flexible canes that will more easily

An arbor *bedecked with the Modern Climbing rose 'America' creates a visual fanfare that introduces the steps leading up to this home.*
(Pat Welsh garden, Del Mar, CA)

Ramblers, as a class, are healthy plants that don't require much protection from pests, diseases, or the cold.

bend over the top of an arbor and hang down in pretty ways, making their blossoms more visible from below. Their laterals are also lax and are the desired form for arbors—and for archways and pergolas, for that matter. Ramblers, as a class, are healthy plants that don't require much protection from pests, diseases, or the cold. However, hardly any Ramblers are rebloomers, so you'll have to admire them for their single show.

For a season-long display on an arbor, try combining several roses. Run a Rambler up one side to cover the top, then cover its bare trunk with shorter Climbers or Shrub roses. Another short rose can be planted on the opposite side of the arbor for color from the ground up. Some beautiful Climbers, including some strongly reblooming Hybrid Teas, only reach 7 or 8 feet. Stagger their young canes as mentioned above. If you choose different varieties for the same arbor, carefully coordinate their colors so that they harmonize. Use the boldest colors closest to the ground if there's a strong differentiation, or intermingle lighter and deeper, related shades together.

You can also combine Ramblers with perennials. For instance, if your gateway arbor is topped with a pink or red Rambler, make sure a few lax canes come over a side where you've planted blue *Delphinium* (both the Elatum Group and Pacific Coast hybrids will work). The blue, 5- to 6-foot, majestic spires reach up as the red or pink roses come tumbling down toward them, perhaps mingling in places. The sight is extraordinarily beautiful.

On many properties, the area along the side of a house is a short, narrow passageway leading from a generous front yard to an even larger backyard. An arbor attached to the house and topped with roses can turn this uninteresting stretch into a delight. Just be sure the area will receive enough sunlight for your roses.

Embracing a Pergola

A pergola is actually a series of arbors strung together to make a long, colonnaded structure. It often enhances a walkway, and easily becomes the most dominant element in just about any landscape—especially when it's dressed in glorious roses. The pergola should begin and end at defined points or features in the landscape, even if that's just from one end of a garden to the other. In fact, the perimeter of a garden is actually a good place for a pergola, where someone walking under it would be able to look into the garden, seeing it as a series of pictures framed by the pergola's rose-covered pillars.

Roses climb *the supports of a formal, rectangular pergola and strew the pathway below with petals. Such a structure gives a classic, formal look to the landscape.*
(Ellsworth garden, Yountville, CA)

A series of metal arches curves to form an informal pergola. The Modern Climbing rose 'Alchymist' graces the pergola, which shades the Lutyens bench below. (Douglas garden, Baton Rouge, LA)

Leave Some Structure Showing

It's not appropriate to completely cover the pergola with roses. Doing that creates a very shady interior where no roses will bloom. They'll all be on the sides and top, mostly unseen by anyone walking inside the pergola. The shape of the structure should be partially seen between the billows of roses. It's the contrast of the sturdy structure of the pergola with the natural tumble of roses that gives the most impressive effect. With no roses, it's an empty pile of wood. With no structure, it's an overgrown jumble of thorny canes. Somewhere around one-half roses and one-half wood is ideal. This may mean planting Ramblers and Climbers along opposite sides and doing some judicious pruning in the dormant season.

Although many pergolas are built down a straight path, they can also curve gracefully as they go, especially along the perimeter of a curved garden. If used to divide a garden, the pergola should be bordered with enough lawn so that it can be fully seen from outside, and the garden it divides can be seen from inside. However, a green, grassy swath is not always the best choice for ground cover beneath the pergola. As vines cover the pergola, it will tend to get too shady for most grasses. And because people tend to walk down the middle when they pass beneath a pergola, a bare path often gets worn down the center. Instead of grass, build a 5-foot-wide walkway through your pergola. While a brick or stone path would be eye-catching, crushed gravel or shredded bark are also excellent choices for surfacing because they are affordable and easy to install. The pathway has the added benefit of drawing your eye from one end of the pergola to the other.

Perfect Proportion for a Pergola

The Golden Section, a geometric calculation first used by the Greeks, refers to the point on a line at which the ratio of a shorter section to a longer section is the same as the longer section to the whole line. Mathematically, that point falls at 0.618 along any line given a value of 1. Buildings, such as the Parthenon, that were designed using this principle are considered perfectly proportioned. While it may sound complicated, the Golden Section is really quite simple and can be used to design a pergola.

The height of a pergola's pillars should be 0.618 of the distance between them. If the pergola's pillars are set 12 feet apart, multiply 12 by 0.618 for a pillar height of just under 7½ feet. If the distance between pillars is 15 feet, the pillars should be approximately 9¼ feet tall. Distances less than 12 feet reduce the overhead height too much, and greater than 15 feet result in a pergola that is too large for most residential sites.

A pergola's width should be the same as the distance between the pillars (along the sides). As you view the pergola from one end, the frame will be a perfectly proportioned rectangle. (If the width matched the height of the pillars, it would simply be square, which is less pleasing to the eye.)

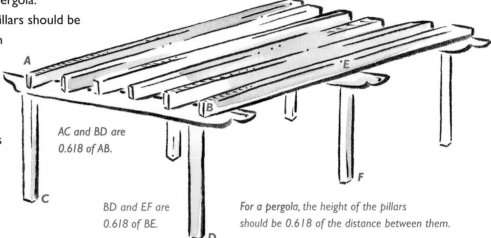

AC and BD are 0.618 of AB.

BD and EF are 0.618 of BE.

For a pergola, the height of the pillars should be 0.618 of the distance between them.

Roses Share the Pergola

The general rules of growing Climbing and Rambling roses on arbors apply to pergolas as well. I would only add that it's important to do your pruning on pergolas in late fall, before strong winter and early spring winds whip the loose canes of these lanky roses back and forth, breaking or damaging them.

And like arbors, pergolas don't have to be limited to roses. Other color-coordinated, flowering perennials and vines can grace the structure as well. William Randolph Hearst espaliered all sorts of fruit trees to his

Arbors and pergolas don't have to be limited to roses. Other color-coordinated flowering perennials and vines can grace these structures as well.

mile-long pergola (quite an immense structure, what's left of it), which ran from his mansion at San Simeon, California, along the mountainside with its magnificent view of the ocean below. This was so guests on horseback could pluck fruit, as well as smell the roses, as they rode through the pergola.

Gracing Gazebos

Gazebos have a Victorian charm that suggests a time of men in white linen suits and women in bustles and bows. While fashions have changed, the charm remains. These stand-alone, round or octagonal, covered outbuildings can be a delightful spot for lunch or a summer snooze, or simply as a phenomenally compelling landscape element.

Gazebos look their best when they have enough elbowroom in the landscape to set them apart from the cluster of main buildings. A good rule of thumb is that they be at least once and preferably twice (or farther) the distance from the house as the house is long. They're best in a secluded spot where they can't be seen from the street or the driveway, and perhaps even partially hidden by plantings when viewed from the house. If yours is out of the way—say, at the edge of a lawn—surrounded by landscaping, with a beautiful view, you have found the perfect spot.

Because gazebos make such a strong architectural statement in the landscape, it defeats their purpose to have them smothered with rampant Ramblers and Climbers. It's much better if they are graced lightly on the south or southwest side with a Shrub rose or two, and a well-behaved Climber twining up one or more of the posts. Roses and clematis may make their most satisfying marriage dressing up a gazebo's sunny roof support.

A gazebo provides a fairy-tale setting for the profuse bloom of 'Climbing Pinkie' and the Polyantha 'Excellenz von Schubert' flowering at its feet. The Verbena below the roses echoes the color of the gazebo's roof. (Michael Shoup garden, Brenham, TX)

Up Pillars and Posts

If roses are used to punctuate the landscape, then a pillared rose is an exclamation point. In fact, of all the ways to use roses in the landscape, I believe growing them on pillars may be the most beautiful. Pillars both balance and contrast with the horizontal flower beds and colorful borders that typically surround them, creating a cheerful setting that lifts the spirits as it lifts its flowers. In doing so, pillars bring roses to eye level, offering not only a better view, but also a cleaner whiff of their fragrance. And the look of a sturdy, erect pillar curled around with a graceful, flower-bedecked rose is romantic and classic.

Anyone with even the most minimal of sunny garden space can grow a rose up a pillar or post, for this combination takes up very little room. And pillars can take the form of a multitude of devices. A tall, classically fluted column is a pillar, but so is a simple 12-foot, 4x4, wooden post (anything smaller might not bear the weight of a Climbing rose) sunk 3 feet into the ground. A slender, metal tower, lamppost, porch post, or the stanchion of a birdhouse or bird feeder can all serve as pillars.

The Climbing Polyantha 'Phyllis Bide' pours its pink and cream roses down a porch post while a lavender clematis climbs up its tall canes. The display is at the corner of the porch—a natural focal point. (Joy and George Wolff Garden, Healdsburg, CA)

Placing Pillars for Impact

If the pillar or post has a primary use other than that of rose support— for instance, as a lamppost, porch post, or birdhouse stanchion—then its primary function will determine where it belongs or already exists in the landscape. If it's a freestanding, decorative pillar—that is, created and

A simple, tall post becomes the underpinning for the Modern Climbing rose 'Blossomtime'. Such pillars give a much needed vertical accent to horizontal perennial beds below.
(Boone Hall, Charleston, SC)

placed in order to receive a rose—remember that it is a dramatic and forceful landscaping element. Place it where you want to draw attention—as a focal point in a mixed bed, at the entrance to a new garden area, or near the end of a fence that is covered with a rambling Multiflora rose.

At the beginning or end of a garden path, a pillar functions as a beacon that says, "Come this way." By a walkway that leads to the front door, it serves as a sign of welcome. In a small backyard, a pillar takes up little room but gives a lot of visual punch. Site it by a water feature, at the edge of a patio, or toward one side of a mixed border. To create a composition that is pleasing to the eye, place it slightly off-center along a walkway or in a garden bed.

Pillars can stand singly, but they are even more dramatic if there are several of them placed along a walkway. An odd number of pillars is preferred to an even number (just like planting odd numbers of perennials in a mass looks more natural), as it makes for a more interesting arrangement. If placed about 10 feet apart, which is a pleasing distance (much closer and they start to interfere with one another, much farther apart and they begin to lose the coherence of a row of pillars), they will not only draw the eye down a pathway, but will firmly insist that you follow.

In Victorian times and before, even in Roman gardens, pillars were often connected by slack lengths of chain fixed near the top of the posts so that the roses could travel horizontally after reaching the top. By planting the same rose at each of a series of pillars, you achieve a formal look. If you change colors as you go, especially if you make radical changes, you get a festive, even gaudy, effect.

Because pillars point skyward, place one just behind the crest of a berm or on a slope, especially where people walking up a set of steps can see it. As one looks up the slope, the eye is caught by the pillar, pleased by the lovely roses that encircle it, and is sent from the top of the pillar to the clouds and blue sky beyond, creating an uplifting vista.

Spiral Roses Up a Pillar

A rose should be trained up a pillar in a graceful spiral. You can bring all canes around in the same direction or train half going one way and half the other. (I like the look of the latter.) Not only do the roses look more graceful spiraling up the pillar than simply climbing it, they present more length of cane to the sun, promoting the development of floriferous laterals, which can be tied in or allowed to spill out and down, as you prefer.

A formal pillar is softened by the nonchalance of the Modern Climbing rose 'Dublin Bay' twining casually around it. A bit of the string used to hold the rose upright and in place can be seen at the pillar's base.

A rose should be trained up a pillar in a graceful spiral.

The ultimate partner *for almost any climbing rose is a large-flowered clematis. This delicious coupling includes the Hybrid Tea 'Climbing Shot Silk' and Clematis 'Gillian Blades'.*

In the case of a classic column, use a Climber that grows only to about 8 feet, and prune it to just a few canes, so that about half to a third of the column can be seen. Prune Climbers in a staggered fashion much like you would for arbors. In winter, cut back a cane or two to just 1 or 2 feet high, another to 6 feet, and a third to 8 feet, so that blooms on new wood will be spaced along the length of the pillar. Because the pillar will be so dominant in the landscape, don't be shy about trimming out the errant shoots as the growing season progresses. Keep your pillars looking trim.

If the pillar is a slender, metal cage (formed from an 8- or 10-foot-long section of rolled hardware cloth), it's easy to tie the canes to the wire mesh. If the post is a slick metal pipe, such as a lamppost, consider wrapping the pipe loosely with plastic garden netting, such as the kind used for pea trellising or deer fencing. It's not seen from a distance, and if the netting is fixed securely at the top, it's easy to tie up the rose canes.

Morning glories (*Ipomoea* spp.), annual sweet peas (*Lathyrus odoratus*), canary creeper (*Tropaeolum peregrinum*), a large-flowered *Clematis* hybrid, a violet trumpet vine (*Clytostoma callistegiodes*), or a well-behaved honeysuckle (*Lonicera heckrottii*) can be paired with continuous-blooming Modern Climbing roses. Keep warm and "sunset" colors like apricot, tangerine, and coral together; pair blue- or violet-flowered vines with yellow, pink, or red roses. A superb combination is the creamy pink Modern Climber 'Clair Matin' paired with the deep, dark red flowers of *Clematis* 'Niobe'.

Attachment Techniques Vary

The method of attaching a rose to a pillar depends on what the pillar is made of. If it's pressure-treated lumber, a few nails driven into the post to which twine or soft ribbon can be tied, then looped loosely around rose canes, should be sufficient to hold the rose in place. If the pillar is made of wood painted white and classic in style—a fluted or straight-sided column, for instance, or a square post with classic ornamentation—then you want to be able to see some of the pillar's design along with the rose. One way to fix the rose to such a column is to place a few small eye hooks near the top and use clear fishing line—which won't be seen at any distance—to make loops of varying lengths that hang down the pil-

A Rose-Covered Birdhouse

A birdhouse placed on a pillar or attached to a wooden fence is the perfect adornment for a climbing rose. Have the rose rise up and surround the birdhouse—the birds will enjoy the habitat. Insect-eating birds will find lunch right outside their door; the thorny canes will discourage cats and possums from attacking the nest; and you will enjoy the delightful sight of a bird, at home, on its perch among the roses.

***Garden structures** of all types improve in appearance when they hold roses aloft. Here a garden swing that extends from an arbor is graced with a Climber, adding romance and beauty to an otherwise drab part of the yard. (Sally Robertson garden, Bolinas, CA)*

The Hybrid Musk *'Lavender Lassie' is planted inside a small tripod, recalling the rustic gardening style of the late 1800s.* (Chris Spindler garden, Calverton, NY)

lar. The rose canes can be suspended with string or twine to the bottom of the loops. Or you can just use eye hooks along the whole height of the wood, though you risk damaging the column over time.

By carefully selecting two Climbers whose colors work together and whose growth habits are relatively modest—to about 8 or 10 feet—two roses can be grown on one pillar very effectively. Spiral one clockwise and the other counterclockwise between the canes of the first. An excellent example would be the disease-resistant, rich red 'Dublin Bay' going one way and the creamy white (with lavender hints) 'Eden Rose 85' the other way.

On Tuteurs and Obelisks

To emphasize a place in the garden, especially a formal garden, obelisks and tuteurs are forms that will give support to twining roses. Pretty in their own right, they are exquisite with the right rose. Generally speaking, obelisks are open structures that come to a point on top, and tuteurs—from the French word for "trainer"—are usually open, spiral cylinders, although they can also be cone-shaped, triangular, or pyramidal. They generally have round tops and crosspieces for tying up roses. While most of these structures are made of wrought-iron or other metal, many of the pyramidal tuteurs are also made of wood. Some are just a couple of feet high and fit nicely in a large pot; others reach to 5 feet or so.

Obelisks and tuteurs are just the right size for elevating short Climbers to eye and nose level, and are especially nice in smaller gardens. They also support tall Shrub roses pruned to a few canes and lax procumbent roses, which can be tied up to them. I'm especially fond of 'Don Juan', 'Pink Perpetue', 'Royal Gold', and 'Blush Noisette' twining their way up an obelisk or tuteur.

Constructing a Rose Tripod

A tripod displays roses well from all sides, and tapers toward the top to give a solid, anchored appearance. These can be placed amid small groups of shrubs or perennials or placed in the lawn as a focal point.

A typical tripod would have three upright legs made of 2x2s spaced 6 feet apart and reaching 8 feet tall. Our high school geometry reveals that the upright legs would each have to be $8\frac{1}{2}$ feet long in such an arrangement. But we want to sink the legs a foot in the ground, so we need legs $9\frac{1}{2}$ feet long.

Plant three roses just inside the legs of the tripod. They should be medium-height roses—those that grow to 6 to 8 feet—with long, arching canes rather than roses with a short, bushy form. Hybrid Musks, Hybrid Moyesiis, and Hybrid Kordesiis are all excellent choices. Three roses of the same kind will cover the pyramid with a solid color and look more stylish and substantial than three different (but color-coordinated) roses. However, mixing single and double roses of different colors will look more interesting and be more fun.

To anchor the legs into the ground, bury three, single-hole, cinder blocks (or three regular cinder blocks if that's all you have), equally spaced at thirds around the base, and just outside the three roses. Bury the blocks so their tops are at soil level. Insert the 2x2 uprights in the cinder-block holes, tilted to they come together at the apex of the pyramid. You may have to tilt the blocks slightly in the hole to accom-

Shrub roses that grow 6 to 8 ft. can be planted at the base of each pole and trained up the tripod.

modate this. Lash the tops of the uprights together tightly with wire, clothesline, or a neutral-colored nylon rope. Then fill the cinder-block holes (with the uprights in them) with concrete, packing it in with a stick so it fills the space completely.

Cut three lengths of $\frac{1}{2}$-inch-thick, 2-inch-wide lathing strips to fit horizontally around the uprights in three places—at 2 feet, 4 feet, and 6 feet above the ground. Because it will soon be covered with roses, a perfect fit and even edges aren't necessary. But if you're looking for a more polished finish, taper the edges so they are flush with the posts. Use a strong staple gun to fix them to the uprights, or tack them in. Roses can be tied to these strips for support. Top the tripod with something unusual and fun—perhaps a large conch shell or colorful glass bowl that you find in your attic or a flea market.

Mulch the ground under the pyramid with pads of newspaper or weed-barrier cloth covered with a thick, 4-inch layer of chipped bark.

And finish by planting colorful annuals or small shrubby plants to hide the legs where they entered the cinder blocks. You could also grow sweet peas or morning glories up the legs to associate with the roses. It will take about three years for the roses to mature and cover the tripod. During that time, trim off any suckers at ground level, keep laterals short for the first two years so the plant's energy goes into the main canes, and use a stepladder to tie them up toward the top. When the roses fill in, it will look very Victorian and lush.

Obelisks and tuteurs are just the right size for elevating short Climbers to eye and nose level, and are especially nice in smaller gardens.

There's something special about the medium-pink roses of the 'Zéphirine Drouhin', which makes Artemisia ludoviciana 'Silver King' at its base a natural companion. Notice the rose's lack of thorns—a feature that makes 'Zéphirine Drouhin' useful for well-traveled locations. *(Peg and Jim Jeffcoat garden, Blythewood, SC)*

These moderately sized, open structures strongly draw the eye, and so are perfect placed at the end of a walkway, between beds, at corners of the garden, or in its very center. Recently a friend wrote to me, saying, "I just loved my 'New Dawn' twining around a tuteur with two blue, small-flowered clematis. Catmint (*Nepeta* × *faassenii*) and star of Persia (*Allium cristophii*) filled in around the base and everything bloomed together in late spring—anchoring the center bed in my formal herb garden."

Along Fences

The prettier the fence, the prettier display roses make on that fence. I'd rank fencing in order of beauty this way: At the top would have to be the horizontal wooden fence, which can take several forms. In one form, upright posts with precut holes accept horizontal rails—usually two of them. Because of the strong visual weight of the fence, Climbers or Ramblers with small roses in profusion give it a pleasing look. In another form, a horizontal wooden fence can be made of split rails, sometimes stacked in the zigzag pattern so often used in the 18th and 19th centuries to enclose pastures. A Multiflora or Polyantha rose would be an appropriate choice for this type of fencing.

Next come the vertical wooden fences, with the white-picket fence giving a traditional look to a front yard. Lax Shrub roses with medium-sized flowers can be wound through the spaces between the pickets to give the rose support. A picket fence has a dainty aspect, so be careful that the rose isn't so vigorous that it grows to the top of the fence and creates a lump of stems, foliage, and flowers that will eventually topple from its own weight. Use modest-sized plants and keep them snipped to cover just a third of the fence. A common type of vertical wooden fence is made from vertical posts and horizontal supports, with vertical boards nailed flush to them. This kind of fence makes a screen, shutting off any view of what's beyond. Here, Climbers or tall Shrub roses with large flowers can be used to climb the fence. They'll need support, such as eye hooks and ties, to hold them to the fencing.

The neat and trim appearance of the salmon-flowered Polyantha 'Margo Koster' seems perfectly suited to the strict regularity of a picket fence. (Lani and Larry Freymiller garden, Solano Beach, CA)

Then come the wrought-iron fences—old-fashioned designs with fleur-de-lis finials or sharp, upright pikes. The soft beauty of roses really improves these. Plant a rose on either side of a gate and tie it to lead away from the gate along a fence. The look will be expansive. Cover no more than two thirds of the fence to retain its structural beauty.

Finally, there are wire fences, from the sturdy chain-link type to something as funky as chicken wire. These fences are more utilitarian than pretty and benefit from being covered with roses over as much of their length as possible. My vegetable garden is fenced with 6-foot-tall range fencing—a sturdy type of wire fence. I've begun the process of planting roses every 10 feet along its inside perimeter, using dark red 'Don Juan' and peachy-pink 'Abraham Darby' alternately. Both roses are richly fragrant and I can't pass 'Abraham Darby', especially, without a whiff of its delicious perfume.

In all cases, training the roses out horizontally on the fence helps them to flower better and it improves the look, too. Very upright roses at intervals along a fence present an awkward sight, while splayed climbers are graceful.

Cover no more than two-thirds of a wrought-iron fence to retain its structural beauty.

TWO

PLANTING
and Caring for
ROSES

Buying Roses ⑤ Growing Healthy Roses ⑤
Planting Roses ⑤ Pruning Roses ⑤ Rose Pests
and Diseases

Buying Roses

Getting your roses off to a good start begins with acquiring healthy, well-grown plants. But first, you must know what roses you are looking for, and with thousands of roses to choose from, that takes a little planning. So before you head off to the local nursery or thumb through the catalogs, think about your landscaping needs:

- Where will your roses be placed? In full sun or partial shade? In a meadow, flanking a pathway, or in a mixed bed?

- What size and form rose plant are you looking for? A 1-foot shrub, a spreading ground cover, a 6-foot bush, or a 20-foot climber?

- What flower color will complement your home or other plantings?

- Do you need a continuous bloomer, a prolific spring bloomer, or perhaps a mix of roses that bloom at different times?

- Will you be able to deadhead, prune, and care for your roses on a regular basis, or do you need low-maintenance varieties that can fend for themselves with only occasional attention?

- What USDA Hardiness Zone do you garden in, and are cold-hardiness or summer heat and humidity important factors for consideration?

Knowing as much as possible about your needs will help you narrow the choices and make your final decision. It will also help prevent impulse buys that often don't work out in the long run.

Hand-Pick Your Roses at Local Nurseries

There are lots of places to buy roses, and some are better than others. If you want to see what you are buying, shop locally rather by than mail order. This is especially nice if want to see the flower color before you buy a container-grown rose. You can also inspect the roses and pick the healthiest plants in the store.

Most local nurseries and garden centers will have a good selection of roses that perform well in your region and a knowledgeable staff to answer your questions. Chances are, they will sell both bare-root roses in early spring and container-grown roses throughout the gardening season. The garden departments at home centers and major discount chains often offer healthy roses too, and at very reasonable prices, though selection is sometimes limited to the most popular varieties. As a general rule, avoid buying roses at supermarkets and drugstores where employees haven't been trained to care for plants.

Shop Catalogs for Greater Variety

By far the widest selection of roses is found in mail-order catalogs. Where local nurseries may have only a few dozen varieties, mail-order firms may offer hundreds. And while most of them

A Healthy Bare-Root Rose

Strong bud union

Fibrous root system

sell healthy plants, you won't know exactly what to expect unless you've dealt with the firm before and they've earned your trust, or until you receive the roses at planting time. If you find a catalog you like, ask your gardening friends if they've ordered from that firm, and what they thought of its service, plant quality, and prices.

A catalog should tell you the grade of the rose, its age at shipping, whether

it's grafted or grown on its own roots, and whether the firm will guarantee replacement if the rose should fail. A catalog may also tell you about its policy for substituting other choices if the rose you ordered is out of stock. Be a little wary of catalog copy that always gushes about each rose without giving any clues to its drawbacks. If a catalog tells you that a particular rose is prone to rust, then you can probably trust its description of the rose's better points.

Buy Bare-Root Roses in Early Spring

Bare-root roses (those from which all the soil has been removed for shipping) are sold in early spring. These dormant plants are usually less costly than container-grown roses because growers can save on shipping weight, but they become unavailable as the weather warms and the roses open their leaf buds. Try to avoid bare-root roses that have already opened their buds into new, reddish growth, and especially those that show lanky, white growth.

Because they lack the root system to support the leafy tops, they can be seriously set back or could even die. For detailed information on how to treat bare-root roses, see chapter 9.

As the plants wake up in the soil, their roots will have a chance to grow fibrous roots and microscopic root hairs that do the bulk of water and nutrient absorption before they are called upon to support a lot of top growth. Local garden-center operators will sometimes plant their bare-root roses into containers of moist sawdust or peat moss so they look like container-grown roses. When replanted at home, the new growth of tiny root hairs will again be disturbed, setting back the plants, so it's best to get bare-root roses early, dormant, and with truly bare roots (usually wrapped in plastic with some moist wood shreds).

Most bare-root roses will be grafted onto different rootstock, another technique that keeps costs down. The rootstock is usually that of a tough, vigorous rose, such as a Multiflora, while the scion—the top part that will bloom for you—is the desired cultivar. These grafted plants are less expensive than own-root roses because they use less expensive rootstock. And since the rootstock is usually more vigorous than the scion's own rootstock, plants can be brought to

market a year earlier than roses grown on their own roots. A cutting of a desired rose may have three to six buds, each of which can be grafted to a separate rootstock, resulting in three to six plants from each cutting. If a cutting is rooted by itself, as in the case of own-root roses, only one plant is created from those three to six buds. However, own-root roses are usually stronger than grafted roses, so don't hesitate to buy them when available.

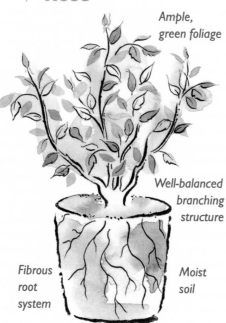

A Healthy Container-Grown Rose

Ample, green foliage

Well-balanced branching structure

Fibrous root system

Moist soil

Buy Container-Grown Roses All Season

Container-grown roses can be purchased at local nurseries and planted anytime during the growing season, as long as drought conditions don't exist or the ground isn't frozen. Unlike bare-root roses, which are grown in a field, these roses have spent their life in a container. You may find own-root roses in containers at your nursery, but more often you'll find grafted plants. Grafted roses will have a knob an inch or so above soil level where the scion has been joined to the rootstock.

When buying container-grown plants at your local nursery or garden center, inspect the individual plants closely.

⑥ Give them an overall inspection. Plants should look healthy, with no black or dying canes. Make sure they don't have any leafless canes, and look carefully at the buds, making sure none are dried out. Reject plants with yellow or spotted leaves.

⑥ Count the canes and assess their thickness. Four canes are perfect; three are acceptable; fewer are suspect. Canes $1/2$ inch thick are perfect; canes between $1/4$ and $1/2$ inch are fine; if they're smaller than $1/4$ inch thick, reject them.

- Look at the shape of the plant. Hold your hand with fingers open, palm up. That's how the plant should look. Avoid those with crossed and crowded stems, and those with stems that grow toward the center instead of outward.

- Check the canes. If they're green, they're healthy; if they're brown, they could be damaged or dying. If the surface is smooth, they're plump with sap. If it's wrinkled, especially lengthwise, they're water-stressed or dying back. Finally, feel them. They should be firm, not soft.

- If you can knock the plant out of the container easily, give the roots an inspection. If they're sparse or broken, or look at all slippery or diseased, avoid that plant. There should be lots of strong-looking roots with plenty of branching. If the plant is severely pot-bound, with roots curling around the outside of the root ball, choose another specimen.

- Check the status of the plant's growth. The red or white growth should look strong, not weak or forced. And if your region is still subject to killing frosts, either avoid anything with green, leafy growth or keep them in their pots and protected until all chance of heavy frost is past.

Roses Are Graded for Quality

To get the choicest roses for your landscape, whether bare-root or container grown, you should know how roses are graded. The grading system is especially helpful when ordering from a mail-order catalog, because you cannot inspect the roses before making a purchase. The American Association of Nurserymen has established the following classification system:

- Number 1—These roses are the best quality. They are strong, vigorous growers that will give you better bloom in their first year and in subsequent years. They have at least three, and often four, healthy-looking canes at least $1/2$ inch thick and 6 inches long.

- Number $1\frac{1}{2}$—These roses have two or three slender canes, and don't appear as robust as Number-1 plants.

- Number 2—These are weak, runty plants that may never grow into robust roses. Don't buy them unless they are varieties you've had trouble finding. You can then take cuttings and root them, handling them carefully so they grow into sturdy stock.

Graded Roses

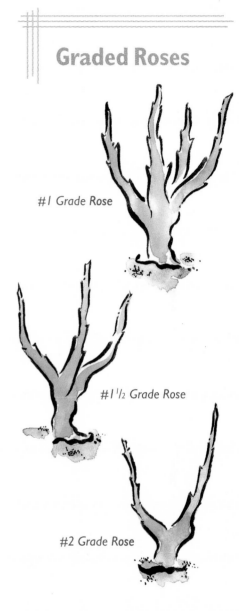

#1 Grade Rose

#1½ Grade Rose

#2 Grade Rose

Most mail-order firms sell Number 1 roses, but ask if they don't specify this in the catalog. Also, make sure that the firm will not substitute a lesser grade if Number-1 grade happens to be sold out. For added insurance, write "Number-1 roses only" on your order form.

Growing Healthy Roses

The first consideration in selecting a site for your roses is, of course, your landscape plan. Perhaps roses are needed growing along a boundary, draped over a fence, mixed with shrubs, lining a sidewalk, or climbing a lamppost. But just because you want to grow a rose somewhere doesn't mean that a rose will necessarily be happy there. Wet, boggy places, for instance, should be avoided for most roses, as should areas of deep shade. But most other situations will work with some modification. For instance, while heavy clay soil is not good for roses, you can amend it by working in lots of organic matter. And in dry climates, you can provide supplemental irrigation. In other words, if you provide the right location and right ingredients, your rose will provide years of beautiful color.

Plenty of Sun

Most roses need at least six hours of sunlight each day to grow and flower properly. Ideally, roses should be sited in places that receive sun all morning and in the first part of the afternoon, if not all day. The farther north you are, the more the plant needs sun all day. In southern regions, where temperatures and humidity are high, roses may benefit from a break from the blistering, afternoon sun.

Sunlight stimulates the plant to produce more leaves, which results in a denser shrub, and to produce more flower buds, which makes the rose more floriferous. Too much shade results in a spindly plant with few flowers and sparsely leaved, long stems. You can change a shady spot to a sunny one, of course, by removing some of the tree canopy overhead. And you can increase light exposure by planting the rose next to a white wall, where reflected light will give it a boost.

If you have otherwise perfect places for roses that receive only four to five hours of sun a day, consider planting one of the shade-tolerant types. Climbing roses, Hybrid Musks, Miniatures, and some Floribundas can get by with fewer hours of sun—although they, too, perform best in full sun.

Chapter 8

Evaluating Your Soil

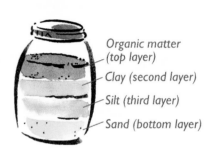

Fill jar one-third full of garden soil.

Add water to fill jar, then screw on lid.

Shake jar vigorously.

Organic matter (top layer)
Clay (second layer)
Silt (third layer)
Sand (bottom layer)

Allow soil to settle; it will separate into different soil components.

Loamy Soil

Roses need a rich, loamy soil that absorbs moisture and nutrients, has plenty of tiny air pockets, is friable enough for roses to spread their roots, and drains quickly enough that those roots are not left standing in soggy soil for extended periods. Since soils vary from one part of the country to another, and because very few of us are blessed with ideal garden soil, we generally have to amend what we have. To do that, it helps to know what we're starting with.

Soil can be primarily clay, silt, or sand, or a mixture of all three. Clay is made up of extremely small particles; silt is composed of larger particles; and sand is the largest of soil particles. If a soil has too much clay, it will be heavy, thick, and poorly drained. If a soil is too sandy, it won't hold water or nutrients. A silt-based soil is the most desirable for roses (and most other garden plants).

To determine your soil type, dig up and loosen a spade-full of soil and soak it with water. Let the excess water drain away until the soil is moist, but not wet. Take a handful of the soil and squeeze it tightly in your hand. Now open your hand. If the soil falls apart immediately into a shapeless mass, you have sandy soil. If it stays together, tap it with the back of your other hand. If it still stays together in a solid mass, you have clay soil. If it gently crumbles apart, you have silty soil.

If this silt is brown and looks a little like coffee grounds, you have a soil rich in organic matter—the ideal soil for roses.

Clay, silt, and sand can all be improved by adding compost (actively decaying organic matter). As compost decomposes completely in the soil, it turns to particles of humus—dark brown, crumbly, nutrient-rich matter like you'd find under the leaves on an old forest floor. When compost is mixed with clay, silt, and sand, it forms a rich, well-drained loam. Give roses 4 to 6 inches of compost each spring before growth starts and in late fall after the roses have gone dormant. This will revitalize the soil with nutrients and, as it decays over winter, improve the texture of the soil. You'll also find plenty of other uses for your compost—from planting to mulching, and protecting tender plants through chilly winters.

Rich Nutrients

Most roses—especially the continuous bloomers—are heavy feeders. The major nutrients—nitrogen, potassium, and phosphorus—are all needed in abundance. Every time you snip off a rose, deadhead a bush, or cut back a stem, you're removing tissue that the plant manufactured from nutrients taken up from the soil. It wouldn't take long for

such a hard-working rose to exhaust the reservoir of soil nutrients, leading to poor, weak, and disease-prone growth.

Species roses can get along with fewer nutrients than our Modern roses because they have evolved to make do with what nature provides in the wild, and that is a steady supply of decomposing leaves and other plant detritus that falls around and under the shrub. But when you grow Modern continuous bloomers in a garden setting and want vigorous growth and lots of flowers, you have to augment what nature provides.

Applying a rose food or fertilizer is one way to improve the nutrient content of the soil. However, I prefer to make my own rose fertilizer from natural materials. Chemical fertilizers are soluble and wash away when it rains.

Also, they generally contain only the macronutrients (nitrogen, potassium, and phosphorus); few of the essential micronutrients—such as magnesium, zinc, and sulfur—are included. A compost-based organic fertilizer will provide necessary nutrients, help make them available to plants longer, and improve soil structure at the same time. Here's my own recipe for organic rose fertilizer:

10 parts compost (either homemade or store-bought)
3 parts composted turkey or chicken manure or 5 parts dried cow manure
2 parts moistened peat moss
1 part bone meal
1 part fish meal
2 parts alfalfa pellets (available at most feed stores)

Quick Guide to Major Nutrients

Nutrient	What it does	Signs of deficiency	Sources
Nitrogen (N)	promotes vigorous, green growth	pale green leaves; stunted or spindly growth	composted manure, high-nitrogen fertilizer, blood meal, alfalfa, soybean meal
Phosphorus (P)	promotes strong root growth	dull or yellowed young foliage; slow plant growth	compost, ground-rock phosphate, bonemeal, super phosphate
Potassium (K)	aids in proper development of flowers and hips; helps plants transport nutrients	leaf discoloration, including brown blotches; leaves may curl; not common in roses	compost, wood ashes, high-potassium fertilizer, alfalfa, granite dust, greensand, kelp, soybean meal

Mix and moisten these ingredients, and use them as a topdressing around roses in spring as they break bud, in midsummer after flowering, and in fall about a month before heavy frost is expected. To keep rose vitality at its peak, drench the dressed area under your rosebush with dilute fish emulsion or manure tea each month during summer. You can make manure tea by placing some farm-animal manure on a porous cloth, tying up the ends to make a sack, and then steeping it in a large container of water.

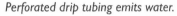

Drip Irrigation Waters Root Zone

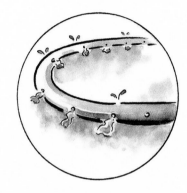

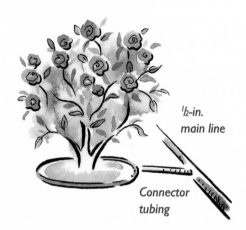

½-in. main line

Connector tubing

Perforated drip tubing emits water.

Slightly Acid pH

The pH of the soil (its relative alkalinity or acidity) is important, too, as it affects a plant's ability to absorb nutrients. A good, rich loam will have a pH between 6.0 and 6.5, which is slightly acidic. At this level of mild acidity, nutrients are most available to the rose's roots for absorption. Fortunately, this is the same pH of compost, so if you've worked a lot of compost into your soil and continue adding compost seasonally, your roses should be in good shape.

Check your soil's pH by taking a soil sample to your local Extension Service or soil laboratory, or by using a soil-test kit that you can purchase at a garden center. If your soil is more acidic than 6.0

(even after working in plenty of compost), work crushed limestone or clean wood ashes into the soil at a rate of about 1 pound per 10 square feet. If your soil is more alkaline than 7.0, add decayed pine needles at the same rate, or gypsum according to package directions.

Ample Water, Good Drainage

Roses like a lot of water, but they don't like wet feet. That may sound like a contradiction, but it's not. Roses need moisture on a regular basis—at least 1 inch a week—but they'll get root rot and die if they're left in standing water for long.

Two conditions create poorly drained soils. The first is heavy clay,

which can be improved with lots of sand, organic matter, or a combination of the two. The other is a low-lying area where water collects. No amount of amendment is likely to help here. Only regrading or installing a system of French drains will correct this problem. So unless you're willing to invest in these options, avoid planting roses in boggy or excessively wet areas.

In many parts of the country where summers are dry, it is necessary to provide supplemental water. Because roses are prone to leaf diseases and molds like black spot and anthracnose, which are encouraged when leaves stay wet, the proper way to water a rose is to deliver the water to the roots, not the tops of the plants. Drip irrigation is an excellent and efficient option, but you can also water by hand with a hose if you avoid spraying the leaves. Water deeply, rather than frequently. This will encourage the plant's roots to strike more deeply into the soil for water, rather than creep out into the top few inches of soil that dries out quickly. The best time to water is morning, so that the humidity from the wet soil surface will evaporate during the day and the plant's leaves will enter the cool night as dry as possible.

With roses, under-watering is preferable to overwatering. They can take a little lack of moisture better than they can a soggy soil. To see if your roses need to be watered, dig into the soil near the canes. If the top 2 inches of soil are dry, it's time to water.

Mulch for Protection

Mulching—applying a layer of organic matter around the base of the plants—is one of the best things you can do to ensure healthy, happy roses. There are many reasons to mulch your roses:

- A thick mulch smothers weeds, unless the mulch itself contains weed seeds. The most common sources of weed-seeded mulch are composted horse and cow manure from animals that have been eating weeds and grasses with ripe seeds in them, and hay that contains ripe seeds. Just make sure your mulch is made from weed-seed-free materials. Fresh manures (those that haven't composted) are too nitrogenous and can burn, stunt, and even kill roses with their superabundance of undigested, water-soluble, nitrogen compounds.

- Mulches protect the life in the soil surface. Where sunlight hits soil, microorganisms are killed. These microorganisms are beneficial and mulch covers the soil and protects them.

- Mulches help keep the soil from drying out. Mulched soil is not exposed to the heat of sunlight and drying winds, and will retain water much longer than bare soil. This means you water less frequently.

- Mulches add nutrients and humus to the soil as they decay. Organic mulches need to be refreshed every spring, and if possible, in late summer as well. That's because mulches are actively decaying organic matter—the secret of a high-nutrient, friable soil. As the mulch is digested by microorganisms, it slowly disappears and needs to be reapplied.

- Mulched soil is cooler in summer—a boon to roses whose roots don't like overly hot conditions. In the winter, mulches keep the soil warmer, often preventing the alternate thawing and freezing that can damage rose roots.

- Mulches prevent rainwater from splashing soil onto the leaves of roses. Bare soil may contain fungus, mold, and disease spores that reach

Mulching a Rosebush

Mulch extends to drip line.

Leave soil bare at stem.

rose leaves when they are spattered upward by raindrops. Mulches break the action of rain and prevent such splashing.

⑥ Mulches improve the appearance of roses. A nice layer of mulch provides a dark background for roses, and mulch just looks better than bare soil.

There may be some disadvantages to mulch, depending on where you live. In the Pacific Northwest, for example, there is a soil pest called symphylans that can breed in mulch, feeding on the decaying organic matter. Similarly, slugs, earwigs, and pill bugs may breed in mulch, too. Even so, the benefits of mulch far outweigh the potential drawbacks. If you're concerned about these issues, ask local rose growers about their experiences and recommendations.

Some mulches are almost purely carbon compounds with little or no nitrogen. Others combine carbon and nitrogen. High-carbon substances like sawdust, dry leaves, and shredded bark tend to use up nitrogen in the soil as they decompose. This is a minor problem, however, and it can be addressed by adding a little extra nitrogen fertilizer

Quick Guide to Mulches

Mulch	Description and benefits
Cocoa bean hulls	An attractive mulch that creates an excellent dark background. The hulls contain some nitrogen and will not deplete the soil of this major nutrient as they decay. They crunch underfoot and smell like chocolate when fresh. They are fairly loose, so they need to be applied—8 inches or more—to suppress all weeds.
Compost	Possibly the perfect mulch. Compost is dark, very nutritious, and will keep feeding the plants through the growing season. It also holds water like a sponge. Apply 6 inches to control weeds.
Grass clippings	A high-nitrogen mulch. Use your own or scavenge clippings from neighbors or golf courses. Just make sure the grass hasn't been treated with a broadleaf herbicide, or you can damage your roses. The clippings will turn black and gooey if they are laid down in thick mats, so they're best applied in a 3-inch layer by shaking them loosely. Grass blades age to a pleasant tan color, and they add nutrients to the soil as they decay.
Leaf mulch	An excellent mulch. Very nutritious for the soil and good-looking, too. Save dead leaves in large bags in the fall and use them as mulch when roses are uncovered in spring. Shredded leaves are best; whole leaves will mat and don't look as good. Spread 3 or 4 inches thick.
Peat moss	If peat moss is wet and dense, it can be a good mulch if applied to a depth of 3 or 4 inches. When it's dry and fluffy, however, weeds will grow right up through it. It helps to improve soil structure, but has little nutritional value.
Pine straw	Pine straw is acidic, which can ameliorate a neutral or alkaline soil. It will also add plenty of humus to the soil as it decays. Spread it 4 or 5 inches deep for an attractive, brown mulch.
Shredded bark	Another excellent mulch. It looks good, and if applied 6 inches deep, will prevent weed growth. It will eventually break down into humus and improve the soil. Keep in mind that you'll need to add extra nitrogen to the soil.

to the soil to compensate. As an alternative, choose a mulch that has its own source of nitrogen. Grass clippings and other green materials have as much nitrogen as cow manure, for instance. Or mix a source of organic nitrogen such as alfalfa pellets, composted poultry manure, blood meal, or fish meal into a high-carbon mulch.

If weeds are a major problem and mulches alone don't do the trick, you might consider adding a weed barrier beneath your mulch. These are impenetrable materials that are spread on the ground to kill or help prevent the growth of weeds. While they do help keep weeds under control, they can sometimes limit the amount of water and decaying mulch that can reach plant roots below. For this reason, you might limit your weed barriers to paths and areas between plants, but leave the ground directly beneath your roses mulched only. The most notable weed barriers include:

⑥ Newspapers—Use thick sections of the daily paper. Avoid the slick "magazine" inserts.

⑥ Old rugs—Woven cotton rugs without plastic backing are the best choice, as the natural fibers will eventually break down and add a bit of humus to the soil.

⑥ Plastic—Sheets of black plastic control weeds very effectively, but in sunny areas, they can heat the soil to extremes. Also, when they eventually break down, little pieces of plastic are scattered in your beds, so replace them every few years.

⑥ Barrier ground cloth—Because they are made of woven threads, they allow some moisture to reach plant roots. Like plastic, however, they will eventually shred and should be replaced every few years.

Protection from Wind

If you live in an area subject to high winds, look for a sheltered spot where the roses will be protected. Winds can damage leaves, dry out new growth, and work the stems back and forth, loosening the plant in the soil. Where prevailing high winds are from the west, plant roses on the east side of a tall windbreak such as a high fence, a tall hedge, or the woods' edge. In the Sunbelt, this site has the advantage of shading the roses in the afternoon. Just make sure the roses are far enough from the windbreak that they aren't shaded too early in the day, especially in the upper portion of the country.

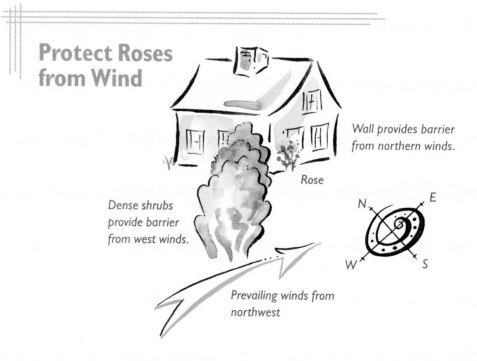

Protect Roses from Wind

Wall provides barrier from northern winds.

Rose

Dense shrubs provide barrier from west winds.

Prevailing winds from northwest

Planting Roses

Chapter 9

O nce you've selected your site, amended your soil, and purchased your roses, it's time to plant. Planting holes for all roses should be at least 2 feet wide and 18 to 24 inches deep. This is because roses are such heavy feeders that if the planting hole is cramped, the roots will soon penetrate the surrounding soil, which usually doesn't have the kind of nutrition roses need. A generous hole can be packed with nutritious composts and soil amendments while giving roots plenty of room to grow. Beyond digging a generous hole, the technique for planting bare-root roses and container-grown roses varies slightly.

Planting Bare-Root Roses

The best time to plant bare-root roses is when they are still dormant, and this can be done prior to the last frost. Catalog companies ship dormant, bare-root roses as the last expected frost date is approaching. When they arrive, you'll want to unpack and plant them immedi-

ately. If you purchase bare-root roses from the local nursery, purchase them as soon as they arrive at the nursery and get them in the ground before they leaf out. If they are already showing signs of growth, you can still plant them, but be cautious. A killing frost will nip the new growth and set the plants back. If you're faced with this situation, cover your plants with a cardboard box for protection until the danger of frost passes. Dormant plants, even if they've just been planted, can usually handle a late cold snap without protection.

As a general guideline, bare-root roses should be planted:

- 🌀 *Early February to mid-March (Zones 9 and 10)*
- 🌀 *Late March to mid-April (Zones 7 and 8)*
- 🌀 *Late April to mid-May (Zones 5 and 6)*
- 🌀 *Mid- to late May (Zones 2 to 4)*

As soon as your bare-root roses arrive, take them out of their shipping box, remove any plastic wrapped around the roots, trim the main roots

Planting a Bare-Root Rose

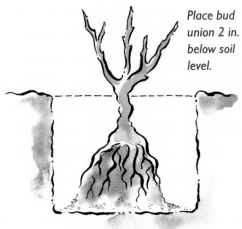

Place bud union 2 in. below soil level.

Spread roots over mound.

back by one-third, then place the plants into a bucket of water up to the bud union (the lump on the stem where the scion is grafted to the rootstock). They can stay in the water for up to a day.

If for some reason you can't plant your roses within 24 hours, heel them in. To do this, dig a trench somewhere in your garden, lay the roses in the trench at a 45-degree angle with their roots below ground and their tops exposed, shovel some soil over the roots, and water them well. Raised beds, with their loose, nutritious, friable soil, are perfect places to heel in roses. They can stay heeled in for a week (or two at most) until time is found to plant them. But don't delay too long, for when heeled-in roses start to grow, they'll grow straight up from that 45-degree angle, which will give them a funny tilt when they are finally moved to their permanent home. The main purpose of heeling in is to keep the roots strong, healthy, and moist. Bare-root roses left in their original packing material will dry out quickly; if watered, they'll tend to rot.

To plant bare-root roses:

1. Dig a large hole (2 feet wide and up to 2 feet deep), and mix the excavated soil with an equal amount of compost.

2. Place 3 or 4 inches of compost in the bottom of the hole.

Heeling In

Roses laid at angle

Trench

3. Place a softball-sized stone in the center of the hole, and cover the stone with a cone-shaped mound of the soil mixture. As an alternative, you can just mound up the soil in the middle of the hole, but make sure it's tightly packed so the roots won't settle.

4. Take the bare-root rose from the water and set it on top of the cone, with the roots splayed out in all directions. Set the plant deep enough so that the bud union will be 2 inches below the soil surface once you've filled the hole. Because buried rose stems

send out roots, burying the bud union allows the scion to root. (Remember that roses are grafted for reasons of economy, not because the rootstock is preferable to the rose's own roots. As the scion roots, the plant will become established on its own roots.)

5. Fill the hole with more of the soil mix, pressing it down lightly into the hole as you go. Continue filling the hole until it's level with the surrounding soil.

6. Water it in well. The new soil mix will settle a bit, creating a slight depression around the plant that will hold water when you irrigate.

Planting Container-Grown Roses

Container-grown roses can be planted anytime during the growing season. However, container roses planted in early spring will establish themselves in the garden more quickly than those planted in summer; those planted in fall, unless they are root-bound, are the easiest to establish of all. Fall is a great time to plant roses, especially in warmer climates, because they put their energy into growing roots that can support the following spring's top growth. Just make sure that they get planted early enough to establish some roots before the soil freezes, and make sure that they aren't root-bound when you buy them. Container roses purchased in summer usually need intensive care to become established during hot, dry weather.

Once again, you'll need to dig large planting holes for your container-grown roses. However, you won't have to splay the roots like you do for bare-root roses. To plant a container-grown rose:

1. Water your rose well. In fact, it's a good idea to place the rose—container and all—into a large bucket of water for an hour before planting to let it soak.

2. Dig a large hole (2 feet wide and up to 2 feet deep), and mix the excavated soil with an equal amount of compost.

3. Fill the hole with water and let it seep into the surrounding soil.

4. Place 3 or 4 inches of compost in the bottom of the hole.

5. Remove the rose from the container, keeping the root ball as intact as possible. Do this even with fiber pots that claim they can be planted with your rose; your roses will establish

themselves much quicker if they don't have to wait for this fiber pot to break down.

6. Inspect the root ball for damaged and molded roots, and trim away such imperfections. If the root ball is white with small feeder roots, use a pocket knife to slice down the root ball's surface every few inches around the circumference, then scratch the root ball with your fingers to loosen up those pot-bound roots.

7. Set the plant in the hole so that the bud union is 2 inches below the soil's surface. If it is too low in the hole, add compost until it's the right height. Fill around the root ball with soil mixture, pressing down as you go, so that the hole is filled to the surrounding soil level. If you purchased an own-root rose, plant your rose at the same level that it was growing in the pot.

8. Water it in, allowing the soil to settle. This will leave a slight depression, or a well, around the canes that will hold water when you irrigate.

9. Finish with a top-dressing of 4 to 6 inches of a compost-based, organic fertilizer mix, and cover the area around your rose with mulch.

Planting a Container-Grown Rose

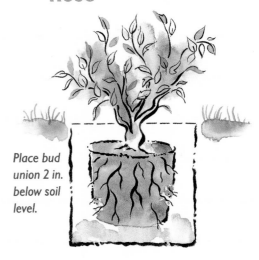

Place bud union 2 in. below soil level.

Planting Roses in Containers

Many roses, especially Patio and Miniature varieties and modest Climbers, will grow nicely in containers. The first key is selecting a suitable container. Any type of container will do—plastic, terracotta, ceramic, or other style—as long as it is large enough to handle the root system of the rose as it grows. Start with a larger pot than you need for the young rose so that you don't have to transplant it. A larger pot also retains moisture longer and doesn't leach nutrients as quickly. Make sure your pot has plenty of holes in the bottom for drainage. Here are some other tips for potting up and growing roses in containers:

1. Select a good potting soil. While there are many commercial varieties available, my favorite potting soil is a mix of roughly 60 percent compost, 15 percent sand, and 25 percent vermiculite; exact measurements aren't necessary. The compost provides structure and nutrients, the vermiculite helps retain the right amount of moisture, and the sand helps with drainage.

2. Place several inches of soil mix into the bottom of the pot. Loosen the root ball and place it into the pot. Grafted roses should be planted with the bud union an inch or two above soil level; own-root roses should be planted at the same depth they were growing in the nursery container.

3. Fill around the root ball with more soil mix, pressing it in firmly as you go. Don't fill the pot to the top with soil; leave an inch or two so you can fill up to the rim when watering.

4. Water frequently. In hot, dry weather, that may mean every day. In cool or overcast weather, every two or three days may be adequate. Pots lose moisture quickly, so be diligent about watering. Water-stressed roses will not bloom well and are more susceptible to pests and diseases. As long as you have good drainage, it's difficult to overwater a container of roses.

5. Fertilize often. Potted roses are heavy feeders, and fertilizer tends to leach out the bottom of pots whenever they are watered. So give your potted roses weekly doses of manure tea or fish emulsion during peak growth and bloom times. Drench them every two weeks at other times.

6. Once every month or so, water the pot until the water runs freely out the drainage holes in the bottom, then water again, and again a third time, to flush any buildup of soluble salts out of the pot.

7. Refresh the soil every year or two. During the dormant season, before the buds break, lift the plant from its pot with a small ball of soil around its roots. Empty out the rest of the soil and replace it with fresh potting mix. Trim off any extra-long roots that curl around the outside of the root ball, then replant the rose and water it well.

Planting a Grafted Rose into a Container

Select pot size for a full-grown rose.

Place *graft union 2 in.* **above** *potting-soil level.*

Transplanting a Rose

Prune rose by approximately two-thirds.

Dig root ball slightly larger than pruned plant.

Transplanting Roses

The best time to transplant a rose is in early spring, while the buds are still tight. An autumn transplant is good if you do it early enough for the roots to reestablish a network of root hairs so the plant can stay hydrated during the winter. This means doing the job before complete dormancy, while most of the leaves are still green. In Zones 5 to 7, this usually falls between September 15 and October 15. If you live in a colder zone, transplant a few weeks earlier, and if you live in a warmer zone, wait a few weeks.

1. Start by trimming back the top growth by about a third.

2. Dig a root ball about 2 feet in diameter with the rose at its center. Slip a spading fork under the roots and lever the root ball out of the hole, retaining as much soil around the root ball as possible.

3. Trim off any old or dead canes and broken roots.

4. Replant the rose in a hole slightly larger than the root ball, at the same depth that it was previously planted.

5. Water well, and continue to water frequently until the rose is reestablished in its new home.

Propagating Roses

When most people think about propagating roses, grafting is usually the first method that comes to mind. However, there are several easier propagation techniques that will give you many rose plants from a single mother plant. One involves taking cuttings from an existing rose and rooting them. The second calls for layering stems still attached to a plant in surrounding soil until it takes root. The third is a modified form of layering. All produce genetically identical, own-root plants. Cuttings will produce more new roses per plant, but layering is a more reliable method.

There are even more ways to propagate roses. Single buds can be grafted onto a rootstock; a scion stem can be grafted onto a rootstock; and seeds from hips can be chilled and planted. Grafting is more often employed by breeders and wholesale nurseries, and your own-root roses will generally result in stronger plants. Starting roses from seed takes longer and will not produce a plant identical to the parent. Therefore, these latter techniques will not be covered in detail here.

It should be noted that most Modern roses are patented for 20 years. These roses cannot be reproduced for sale, but you can propagate them for your own garden.

Propagating Roses from Cuttings

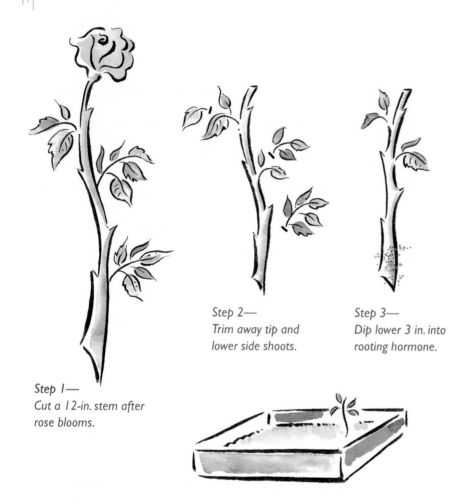

Step 1—
Cut a 12-in. stem after
rose blooms.

Step 2—
Trim away tip and
lower side shoots.

Step 3—
Dip lower 3 in. into
rooting hormone.

Step 4—
Insert 4 in. deep in planting bed; firm soil and water.

Rooting Rose Cuttings

The best time to take cuttings from roses for propagation is from mid-August to mid-September, after roses have finished flowering. The roses will be past their spring rush to flower and reproduce, and the cooler temperatures will treat the cuttings more gently than midsummer. Here's how to take and root these cuttings:

1. Look for healthy, smooth, green canes about the thickness of a pencil that have finished flowering. Cut off the top third or so of each cane (1 or 2 feet is fine), making sure you've got about six or seven leaf buds (small green or reddish bumps where a leaf stem joins the cane) on each. Take the canes to your working area.

2. With a clean, sharp knife, make a 45-degree angle cut just below the bottom leaf bud of each cane. Then make a second, straight cut just above the fifth bud.

3. Cut off any leaves from the bottom three buds. Cut any leaves extending from the top two buds in half, cutting straight across the leaves from side to side. Since the cuttings don't have roots yet, this reduces the amount of leaf surface the cuttings have to support.

4. In a well-amended, raised bed (I recommend a nursery bed devoted solely to propagation), poke 3- to 4-inch-deep holes every 8 inches with your finger or the eraser end of a pencil. (Note: You can also start cuttings in pots filled with potting soil, which are then placed in a warm, but not sunny location. Allow one cutting per pot.)

5. Although it's not necessary, you can dip the angled end of cuttings in a commercial rooting hormone, then tap the canes to shake off any excess powder. Many rose cuttings will root without the hormone, but this should improve your rate of success. Even with rooting hormone, you should be prepared to lose a few of your cuttings, so be sure to root more cuttings than you need.

6. Place the cutting in the hole, angled-cut down, so that only the part with the leaves is aboveground.

7. Firm the soil around the cuttings and water thoroughly. Keep the cuttings constantly moist until they put out roots. This will take about six weeks, and then you can follow a normal watering schedule.

8. Leave the rooted cuttings in the nursery bed until spring, when you can transplant them to their permanent home in the garden.

Layering Rose Canes

Unlike rooting cuttings, where the success rate varies from plant to plant and year to year, I've had almost complete success with layering. However, you can't do much layering from a single rose plant, so it's a technique to use when you just want one or two more roses of the parent type.

1. In late spring, early summer, late summer or early fall, find a long, flexible rose cane that has finished blooming and can be easily bent to the ground without breaking. This is often easiest on lax or procumbent roses, rather than stiffly upright and shrubby roses.

2. Dig a hole about 6 inches long, 3 inches wide, and 4 to 6 inches deep, angled toward the cane so that you can lay the cane down into it with an extra 1 foot of its tip extending beyond the hole.

3. Look on the underside for a leaf bud that will be buried in the hole. With a sharp knife, slice approximately one-third of the way through the cane just beyond this bud (farther out the cane). Bend the tip part of the cane slightly upward so that it forms a wide V, without rupturing the cane any further.

4. Fill the hole with a mix of garden soil and compost, mounding it a little above ground level. Press it down firmly, and place a stone over the trench to keep the cane in place.

5. Water well, and continue to water frequently to keep the soil from drying out.

6. After about two months, the layered cane should root at the cut you made. When new growth has started at the tip end and there's a little resistance when you remove the stone and gently tug at the cane, cut the mother cane where it enters the soil on the side closest to the mother plant.

7. With a spade, cut down into the soil around the trench, root ball, and the protruding cane tip. Lift the new plant and immediately transplant it to its permanent home in the garden.

An Easy, Modified Layering Technique

Rose stems that are buried under the soil for a year will root. You can take advantage of this habit to root new plants from a favorite rosebush.

1. In spring, when the buds are still tight, trim the shrubs back to four or five thick, healthy-looking canes, each about 3 or 4 feet tall.

2. With your fingernail, nick out the buds along each cane from the ground to within a foot of the tip.

3. Mound some rich garden soil (mixed half with compost) up over the plant so that only about 2 feet of the canes are showing above soil level. Add soil as needed throughout the summer and into fall to keep the bottom foot or two of each cane covered.

4. A good layer of mulch will also help keep the soil from washing away, and will protect the rose through the following winter.

5. The following spring, before the buds begin to open up, carefully remove the mound of soil from the canes. You'll discover that each cane has rooted in the mounded soil.

6. Sever all but one cane from the mother plant, keeping as much of the new root system attached to the cane as possible, and immediately transplant them to their new homes. As you do this, be sure to keep the roots from drying out by keeping them covered and watering immediately upon planting.

7. Mound the soil back up around the remaining cane and roots of the mother plant and allow it to grow back into a shrub.

Propagating by Layering

Bend long cane down into shallow trench.

After roots emerge, sever from original shrub and transplant new rose.

Chapter 10

Pruning Roses

Pruning is the process of removing dead, diseased, suckering, crossed, weak, and old canes from a rose. We do this to keep a rose healthy, to shape it for better appearance, and to encourage the growth of new foliage and flowers. All roses need to be pruned, but some need it more than others. Today's Modern Shrub and Landscape roses, for instance, are billed as low maintenance and, indeed, most don't need to be pruned heavily. But even these roses can use some occasional sprucing up.

For me, pruning roses is one of the most pleasant jobs in the garden. Most of the work is done standing up rather than kneeling, and with each cut, I'm thinking about how the roses will grow and flower.

Making a Pruning Cut

Outward-facing bud

Angled cut just above bud

Prune with Purpose

Despite its reputation for being difficult, pruning is actually rather simple if you know why you're making each cut and how the plant will respond to it. Here are some general pointers that apply to pruning roses:

- Remove any dead, diseased, or weak canes. To prevent the spread of disease, dip the blades of your pruning shears in alcohol between cuts, and discard or burn all infected canes. Do not place diseased canes in the compost pile.

- Examine the center, or pith, of each cane. If it is discolored, prune the cane back to the point at which the pith turns white.

- On shrub roses, remove crossing canes that clog up the center of the bush. This will allow sunlight to reach more canes and will help prevent the development of diseases.

Pruning a Climbing Rose

Pruning a Hybrid Tea

Pruning a Shrub Rose

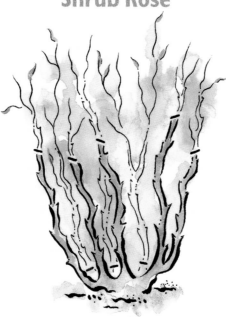

⑥ If you have a grafted rose, remove any suckers that are emerging from the rootstock. You'll notice them at the base of the plant as thin, vigorous, upright canes with seven-leaflet compound leaves. They'll look distinctly different from your other canes. Don't cut these suckers off at ground level, or you'll just encourage twice as many to grow. Instead, dig away enough soil to see where they emerge from the rootstock and, with a pocketknife, cut them out, leaving a shallow depression where they emerged. If you allow these suckers to grow, they'll quickly take over your rosebush, and their flowers will be distinctly different from your cherished rosebush.

⑥ Once-blooming roses flower on old wood, so prune them in summer after they have flowered.

⑥ Continuous-blooming roses flower on new wood, so prune them in late winter or early spring, and deadhead them throughout the summer. Hybrid Teas and other frost-tender continuous bloomers, such as Hybrid Perpetuals and Grandifloras, that are grown in cold climates are an exception. They should be pruned in late fall and mulched heavily for winter protection.

⑥ To prune a rose, cut ¼ inch above an outward-facing bud with bypass pruning shears (which make a cleaner cut than anvil pruning shears). Cut at a 45-degree angle, so that the back of the cut is directly behind the bud.

Quick Guide to Pruning Roses

Rose class	When to prune	How to prune
Hybrid Teas, Hybrid Perpetuals, and Grandifloras	In Zones 7-9, prune in late winter or early spring when about half the buds have swollen, but before they break open into leaves. In colder regions, prune in late fall after they've gone dormant, and provide winter protection with a thick layer of mulch.	Take off ½ to ⅓ the length of young canes, cutting back to an outside bud, and reducing their number to between three and six canes, depending on the vigor of the shrub. Prune off three-year-old or older canes at their base, which stimulates the growth of new canes.
Floribundas	Late winter or early spring before bud break	Cut back the strongest young canes by about ¼ of their length. Remove any three-year-old or older canes. Prune off any weak, broken, or crossing canes.
Miniatures	Late winter or early spring, before bud break	Take off ½ to ⅓ the length of young canes, cutting back to an outside bud, and reducing their number to between three and six canes, depending on the vigor of the shrub. Prune off three-year-old or older canes at their base, which stimulates the growth of new canes.
Polyanthas	Late winter or early spring, before bud break	Focus on removing about ¼ of their twiggy, interior growth, but don't cut the length of canes back by more than ¼.
Once-blooming Old Roses and Modern Shrubs	Midsummer, after flowering	Remove any old or diseased canes, and prune lightly to keep them in shape. Most do not need to be pruned heavily. If you need to renovate an old shrub, prune it as you would repeat bloomers in late winter or early spring, but know that you'll have few blooms that following spring.
Repeat-blooming Modern Shrubs, Bourbons, and Chinas	Late winter or early spring, before bud break	These will bloom on new growth, as well as on laterals of one- and two-year-old canes. Cut back long main canes by ½ and cut back laterals of one- and two-year-old canes to about 6 inches or to include two buds. Remove any three-year-old and older canes at their base, and clean up any weak, broken, crossing, diseased, or out-of-place canes.
Climbing roses	Primary pruning after first flowering, usually in June. Cut back laterals in late fall when plants are dormant.	For the first three years, allow the canes to grow up your structure. Once established, cut back laterals to about 6 in. or to include two buds. For about six years, climbers will send up new canes from their base; cut these back by ½ when they reach dormancy to promote the formation of laterals. On mature climbers, you can stimulate the production of a new cane near the base by cutting a third of the way through the cane just above a low bud near the ground.

Deadheading

Deadheading is the removal of flowers that have finished blooming. Roses look better when spent blooms are removed, and repeat-blooming and continuous-blooming roses are encouraged to produce more flowers. For this reason, the best time to deadhead flowers is immediately after they have finished blooming. Though they won't produce any more flowers, most once-blooming roses look better through the summer if they are deadheaded.

Many roses, though not all, will produce hips (ornamental seed capsules) in the fall if flowers are not deadheaded. If you have a hip-producing variety, consider leaving a late-summer crop of flowers on the shrub. In addition to their ornamental value, hips provide food for wildlife in fall and winter.

You'll notice that with most roses, the compound leaves farthest out the stem have just three leaflets. Farther down the stem, you'll find five leaflets in each compound leaf. To deadhead, cut ¼ inch above the first outward-facing bud where a five-leaflet compound leaf appears. It should be noted that some

Deadheading a Rose

Cut just above a five-leaf compound leaf.

rose growers now suggest that the stem will be more floriferous if deadheaded where it attaches to the cane, regardless of how many leaflets there are on the leaves. Other rose growers disagree. Try pruning some each way and decide for yourself.

Protecting Tender Roses over Winter

Roses have been rated for cold hardiness by the USDA, and these recommendations have been included throughout this book. These are the zones in which the roses should survive without special treatment. Just about all roses will survive in Zones 7 to 9 without protection. You can, however, grow tender roses such as Hybrid Teas, Grandifloras, and Hybrid Perpetuals in colder climates than they are rated for—say, a zone or two colder—by giving them extra winter protection. For those living in cold climates, this expands the choices of roses that can be grown.

The first step in putting tender roses to bed for the winter is to prune them in late fall after they've reached dormancy, instead of in late winter or early spring. Once pruned, there are several ways to bring them through the rigors of winter weather. Here are several options:

❧ Surround them with a cylinder of wire, fill the cylinder to the top with dry leaves, and give it a solid top to prevent ice, snow, and freezing rain from compressing the leaves. (See the illustration on the facing page.)

Hill soil up over the heavily pruned canes, then cover the mounded soil with a thick mulch of straw, hay, or other material.

Take climbers and ramblers down from supports, lay the canes on the ground, and cover them with evergreen boughs. Next, cover the boughs with burlap or an old rug. If mice and voles are a problem in your garden, cover the roses with hardware cloth tucked into the soil on all sides before adding the evergreen boughs.

Shovel a blanket of insulating snow on top of these protective covers, to further shield your roses from low temperatures.

About six weeks before the last frost date, remove most of the winter protection, leaving a small pile of the leaves or hay around the canes. This is a good time to trim off the tips of any canes that were damaged over winter. Two weeks later, after your roses have time to adjust and the weather has warmed a bit more, remove the remaining mulch and give your roses a 3-inch topdressing of compost to get them off to a good start. Once they begin to show signs of growth, you can fertilize your roses.

Winter Protection for a Hybrid Tea, Grandiflora, and Floribunda (in Zone 6 or colder)

Step 1—
Prune in fall,
when dormant.

Step 2—
Slip wire cage
over plant.

Step 3—
Fill loosely with
leaves or straw.

Step 4—
Top with board
and rock.

Note—For added protection in extreme climates, consider adding layer of burlap.

Rose Pests and Diseases

Even with all the new developments in roses, many of our favorites remain prone to diseases and subject to destruction by insects and animals. We can help by choosing pest- and disease-resistant roses and by creating a healthy environment for our roses. We can also tolerate a certain level of damage and use environmentally friendly measures to keep problems under control. Chemicals, if we must use them at all, should be employed only as a last resort. In the long run, replacing roses that have serious pest and disease problems is considerably easier and more environmentally friendly than dousing our yards with chemicals.

R. rugosa hybrids, David Austin's English roses, Dr. Griffith Buck's prairie roses, and the Carefree, Dream, and Flower Carpet series are all noted for their exceptional pest and disease resistance. Many other Modern Shrub and Modern Climbing roses are nearly trouble-free, including 'Dublin Bay', 'Gene Boerner', 'Iceberg', 'Königin von Dänemark', 'Margaret Merril', 'Alba Maxima', 'Pascali', 'Queen Elizabeth', and 'Schwarze Madonna'. Also, keep in mind the many wonderful Old Garden roses, which have been around for centuries—primarily because they've adapted to their environment and won the battle against rose pests and diseases. Check nursery tags for information about pest and disease resistance.

Choose Resistant Roses

One of the greatest advances in rose breeding is the introduction of pest- and disease-resistant roses. Even if you don't use them for all of your plantings, they are good replacements for roses that give you the most trouble.

Prevention Pays

Understanding what causes problems is the greatest key to prevention. Healthy roses often withstand attacks by insects and diseases; unhealthy plants are much less able to cope. Many insects, in fact, are attracted to unhealthy plants over healthy ones, just as a wolf pack will take the weakest stray.

Nutrient-depleted, lifeless soil attracts soil-borne diseases. Dry, dusty conditions draw red spider mites and powdery mildew. Overcrowded plants (whether from being placed too close to other plants or lack of pruning) attract fungal diseases like black spot. The best thing you can do for your roses is give them a happy home. Select a sunny spot, give them plenty of water, and keep them pruned and constantly supplied with actively decaying organic matter—not just to feed the roses, but also to feed the life in the soil. The microorganisms in healthy soil can destroy the spores and eggs of creatures that cause diseases.

The most useful way to identify pest and disease problems with roses is by the symptoms and problems they cause. The use of a hand magnifying glass can help you pinpoint the pests or diseases that are causing the damage. And by checking your roses routinely, you can catch any emerging problems before they get out of hand.

Identifying Common Rose Problems

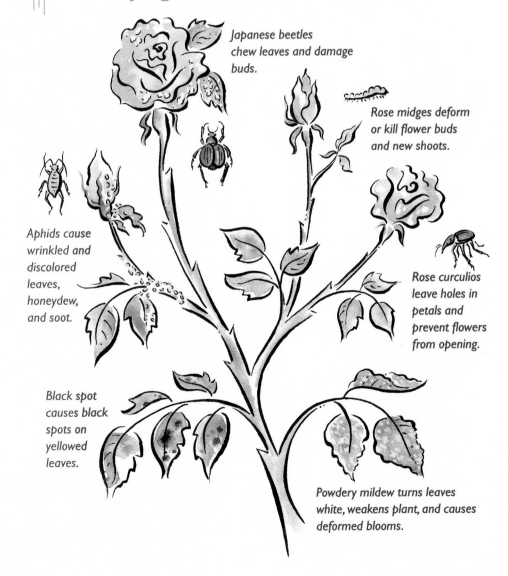

Japanese beetles chew leaves and damage buds.

Rose midges deform or kill flower buds and new shoots.

Aphids cause wrinkled and discolored leaves, honeydew, and soot.

Rose curculios leave holes in petals and prevent flowers from opening.

Black spot causes black spots on yellowed leaves.

Powdery mildew turns leaves white, weakens plant, and causes deformed blooms.

Troubleshooting Pest Problems

Symptom	What it is	What to do
Flower buds and stem tips are deformed or dying.	rose midge larva, which looks like a small, white maggot and can be found buried in the tender tissue at the stem ends or buds	Prune infested stem tips back to the healthy part of the cane.
Stem tips die, and you don't see any rose midge larvae.	rose cane borer, which will create a neat hole somewhere on the stem tip, usually near where the damage begins	Prune the dead tip back to healthy tissue and slice open the stem from the hole toward the tip. If you find a hollow stem and a little grub in there, that's the cane borer. Prune away all infected canes. Plug the ends of the canes with grafting wax or wood glue.
Canes are swollen, with spiral channels around them.	stem girders	Prune away infected tissue.
Flowers proceed to bud stage, but fail to open; petals have brown edges, flecks, and streaks, and the bud looks damaged.	thrips, which are tiny, slim, yellowish-brown insects	Prune away all infected stem tips and buds. Spray weekly with neem extract and/or insecticidal soap. Systemic pesticides are also effective (but don't use any part of sprayed roses for potpourri, candied rose leaves, or food garnish).
Leaves have neat round, oval, or half circles cut out of them, and stem tips are wilted.	leaf-cutter bees	Leaf damage usually isn't extensive enough to warrant treatment, but they also lay eggs inside the tender stem tips, causing them to wilt. Prune wilted portions back to good wood and plug the tips with grafting wax or wood glue.
Wrinkled young leaves and tender stem tips are covered in tiny, pear-shaped bugs.	aphids, which are soft-bodied sap suckers; they excrete a sticky "honeydew" that attracts ants and is soon covered in a black soot.	Spray them off with a strong blast of water every few days; spray with insecticidal soap; or release green lacewing larvae or ladybugs.
Leaves are skeletonized and holes appear in petals; larger, rounded beetles with copper-colored wings can be seen.	Japanese beetles	Use neem extract to ward off the beetles. Do not use Japanese beetle traps, which will only draw more beetles to your property.
Leaves are skeletonized and holes appear in petals; very small, sluglike larvae can be seen.	sawflies or rose slug	Spray with insecticidal soap. Do not handpick, as they contain a compund that can irritate skin.

Symptom	What it is	What to do
Buds and leaves have holes in them and buds don't open.	rose curculios, which are $1/4$-inch, red weevils with black beaks; or rose leaf beetles, which are $1/8$-inch, blue, or green beetles	Pick pests off by hand if there are just a few; otherwise, spray with pyrethrin.
Leaves are skeletonized and holes appear in petals; tiny, $1/3$-inch-long beetles can be seen.	rose chafers	Pick rose chafers off by hand or spray with pyrethrin. Kill larvae by applying milky spore disease to nearby lawn areas.
Leaves are dotted with yellow spots and tiny webs, especially on the underside of leaves.	spider mites	Spray both sides of leaves with insecticidal soap; apply summer oil (also called superior oil) in early summer; or release ladybugs.
Leaves and stems have small, brownish lumps or cottony masses; plant surfaces may be covered in honeydew and soot.	scale insects, which are sap suckers	Release ladybugs as a natural predator; spray heavy infestations with dormant oil in winter and summer oil in summer, and prune away badly deteriorated canes.
Leaves eaten or skeletonized.	caterpillars, which can be pests or larvae of desirable butterflies	Unless extensive damage has been done, leave it alone. If a serious problem exists, apply *Bacillus thuringiensis* (Bt), but remember that it will kill both pests and butterfly larvae.

Keeping Pests in Check

One of the best things you can do in most cases of pest damage is nothing. That's because most rose pests have natural enemies that keep the problem in check. Just keep an eye on things, and learn to tolerate a little bit of damage. In many cases, picking off the predators will eliminate your problems. If you remove damaged canes, flowers, or foliage, either burn them or place them in the trash; do not add them to your compost pile.

Keeping Diseases at Bay

While you might put up with a little damage from pests, it's more important to stop a disease before it spreads to other roses. In many cases, you can simply prune away and destroy infected canes or leaves.

Other times, you may need to get rid of an entire plant. Be sure to burn or discard the diseased foliage, canes, or plants; do not place them in your compost pile. If you know that certain problems are common to your climate or the roses you have chosen, spray your roses with elemental sulfur or a baking-soda solution on a regular basis as a preventive measure.

You can make your own soda solution by mixing 1 tablespoon of baking soda (sodium bicarbonate) with 1 gallon of

Troubleshooting Disease Problems

Symptom	What it is	What to do
Canes have dead and discolored patches.	canker, which is a fungal disease	Prune away and destroy any infected canes; spray the plant weekly with elemental sulfur.*
Flower buds are produced, but they don't open. Instead, they turn brown and mushy.	*Botrytis cinerea*, a fungus that is caused by too much moisture and humidity	Trim off any infected stem tips and spray weekly with baking-soda solution or elemental sulfur.*
Canes are swollen, with rough, brown, corky masses near the ground.	crown gall, a soil-borne bacterial disease that enters rose tissue where it's fissured by frost or damaged in some way	Prevent by covering the soil around rose canes with a thick layer of soft mulch, like shredded bark, which prevents raindrops from splashing soil on canes, and be careful not to damage canes when planting. Once established, crown gall is incurable; remove and destroy the plant.
Irregular black spots appear on leaves and stems, often surrounded by yellow patches.	Black spot, a fungal disease found most often on Hybrid Teas, Floribundas, and Grandifloras	Mulch right up to the canes to prevent spores from splashing on the rose leaves during heavy rain. Water the roots, but don't wet the leaves of plants. Pick off infected leaves, remove any fallen leaves, and cut off infected stems. Prevent by spraying weekly and after rains with a baking-soda solution. Once established, dust weekly and after rains with sulfur.*
Red, brown, or purple spots with grey centers; shot holes may appear on leaves.	anthracnose, a fungal disease	Mulch right up to the canes to prevent spores from splashing on the rose leaves during heavy rain. Water the roots, but don't wet the leaves of plants. Pick off infected leaves, remove any fallen leaves, and cut off infected stems. Prevent by spraying weekly and after rains with a baking-soda solution. Once established, dust weekly and after rains with sulfur.*
White, powderlike substance on leaves.	powdery mildew, which first appears on young leaves and spreads to older leaves	Space and prune plants for good air circulation. Prune away and destroy all infected parts. Spray weekly with elemental sulfur.*
Orange-red dots appear on the undersides of leaves and spread to their topsides.	rust, which is especially prevalent on the West coast	Prevent with a weekly application of elemental sulfur.* Once infected, pick off the affected leaves, remove any fallen diseased leaves, and burn them.
Leaves show yellow-green mottling; if not treated, it leads to stunted growth, curled leaves, malformed buds and flowers, and declining vigor.	virus, which is spread by insects—especially leafhoppers and cucumber beetles	Prevent by purchasing virus-free stock and disease-resistant plants. Immediately remove virus-infected plants and destroy them.

*Avoid spraying with elemental sulfur when temperatures are above 85°, as this could burn your rose leaves.

warm water. More is not better, as a stronger solution can burn and even kill leaves. Mix well, then spray weekly and after rains to both sides of rose leaves to prevent fungal diseases like black spot and powdery mildew. To help the baking-soda solution coat the leaves evenly, add 1 tablespoon of insecticidal soap to the gallon of solution. (Do not use dish-washing liquid, which may damage leaves. And avoid adding fish emulsion or con-centrated liquid seaweed to the water, as they could counteract the alkalinity of the baking soda.) If fungal diseases are already established, use elemental sulfur, com-mercial lime-sulfur, or Bordeaux mixtures prepared according to package directions. These products, along with the insecti-cidal soap, are available at garden centers.

Deterring Deer, Rabbits, and Gophers

Roses make a most luscious meal for deer and rabbits. So luscious, in fact, that they can eat rosebushes down to the ground. In the West, gophers will eat rose roots up to the ground, completing the predation. Occasionally, burrowing animals such as groundhogs, mice, and voles will nestle among a rose's roots, but their damage is infrequent and usu-ally just by chance. It's the deer, rabbits, and gophers that need attention.

Deer are the biggest problem. I've found the perfect solution to be a large, protective, female dog that has the run of the property at night. Once the deer know that there's a dog patrolling the proper-ty, they'll avoid it. And so will rabbits.

Deer fencing also works, but it must be at least 7 feet tall, preferably 8 feet to keep deer out. If a 3-foot course of hardware cloth (sturdy, fine wire mesh) is attached to the bottom of the fencing, with its bottom edge buried under the soil, it will also keep out rabbits and gophers. (See the drawing, below.)

I've tried every deer repellent on the market, but none seem to work consis-tently for me. The only other strategy I've found that works is very fine, plastic

netting thrown over plants to protect them. It doesn't look nice up close, but it's effective for roses that are viewed from a distance.

To protect your roses from gophers, plant them in holes lined with hardware cloth fashioned into cages so there is no way for the gopher to burrow inside. A roll of hardware cloth will pro-vide dozens of cages for far less money then commercial cages. Simply cut a square of the wire mesh about half as large as the hole and push it down into the hole until it lines the bottom and sides. Put some soil in the bottom, place the rose in the center, and fill the hole with rich compost and soil.

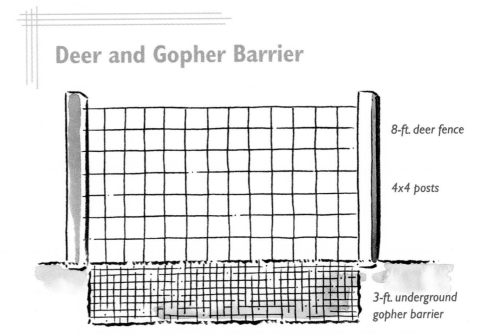

Deer and Gopher Barrier

8-ft. deer fence

4x4 posts

3-ft. underground gopher barrier

USDA Hardiness Zone Map

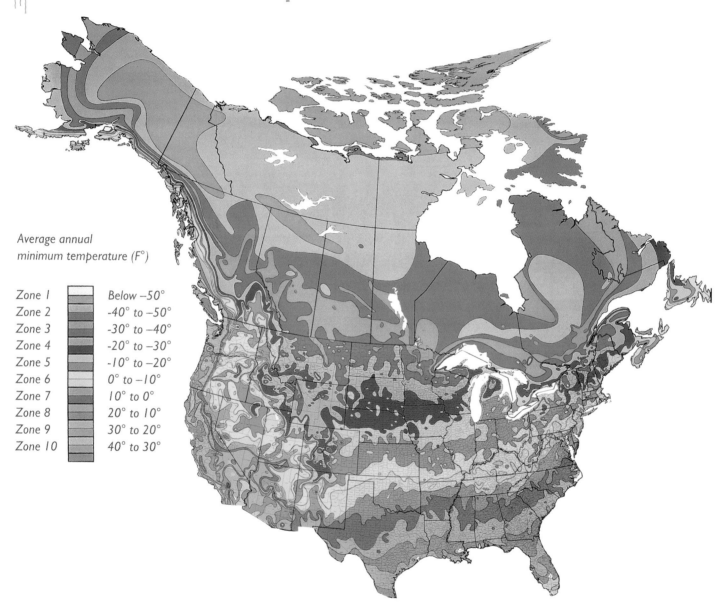

Average annual
minimum temperature (F°)

Zone	Temperature
Zone 1	Below −50°
Zone 2	−40° to −50°
Zone 3	−30° to −40°
Zone 4	−20° to −30°
Zone 5	−10° to −20°
Zone 6	0° to −10°
Zone 7	10° to 0°
Zone 8	20° to 10°
Zone 9	30° to 20°
Zone 10	40° to 30°

Index